*It's Hard to Look Graceful
When You're Dragging Your Feet*

It's Hard to When

The Iowa State University Press / Ames

HELEN FOSTER

Look Graceful You're Dragging Your Feet

Drawings by William D. Lee

© 1983 The Iowa State University Press. All rights reserved. Composed and printed by The Iowa State University Press, Ames, Iowa 50010

No part of this book may be reproduced in any form, by photostat, microfilm, xerography, or any other means, or incorporated into any information retrieval system, electronic or mechanical, without the written permission of the copyright owner.

First edition, 1983

Library of Congress Cataloging in Publication Data

Foster, Helen, 1912–
   It's hard to look graceful when you're dragging your feet.

    1. Foster, Helen, 1912–   2. Aged – United States – Biography. 3. Retirement – United States. I. Title.
HQ1064.U5F63   1983   305.2′6′0924   83-4315
ISBN 0-8138-0811-1

For my grandchildren —

        MATTHEW SHULTZ,

        JONATHAN SHULTZ,

        DEIRDRE COGHLAN,

        AND KIERAN COGHLAN.

*Until they came along,
I doubted there were any rewards in old age.*

CONTENTS

INTRODUCTION *ix*

FROM OVER MY SHOULDER *3*

THE GERIATRIC GAP *14*

HIMSELF *25*

RELATED SUBJECTS *39*

IN THE GLOAMING, OH, MY GOODNESS! *59*

WE'RE GOING TO GET AWAY FROM IT ALL IF IT KILLS US *71*

NOT LIKE THE ONES WE USED TO KNOW *82*

FRIENDS AND FOLKS *89*

OVER *WHAT* HILL? *100*

KEEPSAKES OF MY MIND *115*

POSTSCRIPT *133*

INTRODUCTION

I am old. Not terribly old, just sort of old. I do not like being old.
    Old age sneaked up on me. I know I should have made plans for it, but how does one go about preparing for a catastrophe? While others glided into this phase of their lives, I bounced into mine. Had someone thrown me onto a trampoline, it would not have been a bigger jolt.
    Thomas Mann wrote, "Time has no division to mark its passage. There is never a thunderstorm or blare of trumpets to announce the beginning of a new month or year."
    Maybe I needed a blare of trumpets to warn me that time was running out. But no, I don't think seventy-six trombones could have done it for me.
    I look about me at all the praiseworthy souls who have made the transition into these sunset years with dignity. They are beautiful. On them, wrinkles look good. They never blunder. Every step, every mannerism is calculated. They have grown old gracefully. I wish I were one of them. I tried, but it's hard to look graceful when you're dragging your feet.

*It's Hard to Look Graceful
When You're Dragging Your Feet*

From over My Shoulder

All in a matter of one year, the Keystone Cops made their debut, women discarded their tight corsets, Maria Montessori introduced a new method of teaching children, the Titanic struck an iceberg, Vernon and Irene Castle wowed Paris with their "Castle Walk," and I was born.

Right from the beginning I had hair—lots of it—curly and *red*. The freckles came later. And, still later, my undeniable resemblance to Little Orphan Annie.

Seeing me for the first time, visitors to our home would say, "Oh, dear! Is she going to have red hair?"

This was the cue for my father to usher them from the room with, "Of course she isn't going to have red hair!"

After a time no one asked is she or isn't she. Soon they were offering solace and uttering heartening words like "Well, at least the hair is curly," or "Be glad she's a girl. It's even worse for boys."

Those of us who were blessed with this fiery crown soon learned that it was something less than a glory. We abided the taunts "red-headed woodpecker," "sorrel top," and "carrottop."

There did come a day of deliverance. Elinor Glyn had

written a book called "*It*." "It" was not a pronoun. "It" was a quality, and Madame Glyn set out to find someone who had that quality.

Her search ended with a hot little starlet named Clara Bow. *Clara Bow!* Her eyes were huge, her mouth was tiny, and her knees were dimpled. And—heaven help us—her hair was *red!*

Almost overnight auburn, titian, and chestnut became catchwords, and henna was a staple item in every beauty shop.

Flaming-haired lovelies graced the covers of magazines and sheet music. Suddenly every thrill-seeking flapper wanted what we had always had—a "carrottop."

New doors were opened to us. If this is what it took to have "it," then we had a head start.

My mother, somewhat less enchanted with "it" and the "it girl," never quite understood my earlier aversion to the color of my hair. After all, it *was* curly, and I had good, sound teeth, two hands and two feet, and that, according to her, was about all anyone should ask for.

Mama's hair was brown, and, as she put it, "straight as a string." The top part she would crimp with a curling iron that had been heated inside the glass chimney of a kerosene lamp. The remaining long strands were twisted into a figure eight at the nape of her neck. She was truly a lady, smelling of lavender and Armand face powder.

Yet each year at winter's end, something came over Mama. It always started with a faraway look in her eyes. She would become preoccupied and, seemingly, ill at ease. And then, one morning there she would be, head tied up in a towel, gathering up pails, brooms, brushes, and soap. It was spring housecleaning time and the sergeant was ready for action.

Papa used to say, "If President Coolidge came to call, your mother would say, 'Excuse me, Mr. President, I'm into my spring cleaning.'"

Once he said to me, "Pray for rain, or she'll have you out scrubbing the trees."

This was no time to josh with Mama, so Papa would go off to his work, and leave me wishing I could go with him.

We started in the attic and worked our way down.

From over My Shoulder

Everything that would go through the door was shoved outside to air. Rugs were rolled up and thrown over the clothesline, where they were pounded with the carpet beater. Mattresses, too, were given a whipping as they lay over upside-down kitchen chairs.

Inside, the bare wooden floor that framed the rugs was painted grey one year and tan the next. Wallpaper was cleaned or steamed off and replaced with new. Varnished woodwork was scrubbed, then polished.

Our meals during these days were one-dish affairs and served haphazardly. We went to bed early and arose early. I wondered if I would have any friends left when this was over. I loved my mother – always I loved her, but there were times when she put that love to a real test.

By the time she had set up the curtain stretchers and assigned me to the dreaded task of tugging and pulling the starched lace curtains over each of those little pins, I was sassing her under my breath.

Finally the last of these days of upheaval would be behind us for another year. Everything was back in place – radiant, shiny, glowing, and sterile. The fever had broken and Mama was herself again. Except . . . sometimes . . . she wished she could have something new. "Just some little thing," she would say. "Something to add a little color." Each year we went through this, and each year Mama would settle for painting the birdcage.

It hung in the double window with white crisscross curtains behind it. We saw it change from canary yellow to apple green to Mediterranean blue. I remember best the year it was Chinese red.

Glory be! What I'd give to see anything so pretty and springlike again!

Papa was as relieved as the rest of us when these frenzied days were over. He was at his best when we and everything about us were all in our places with sunshiny faces. He liked things in order, and this included our lives.

When, from time to time, there was distress or dissension, Papa preferred looking the other way. He was a cabinetmaker, and the life he painted for us was as glossy as his freshly varnished tabletops.

When he said, "Go to your room," we went with no

hesitation or remorse. We knew it would be only minutes before he climbed the stairs, tapped on our door, and beckoned us back into the family fold.

Yet he was his own person—unwavering in what he truly believed, firm and unyielding in what he felt was right . . . and wrong. He was companionable, affable, and fun. He was a millionaire with the successful and a pauper with the less fortunate, but he wasn't about to be pushed into any corners. If anyone ever tried, I dare say they never made a second attempt.

After he died, my mother responded to all situations with, "What would your father say?" At first it seemed to be her way of handling her grief. Later it became a fixation—of sorts.

When a relative (on my father's side, of course) failed to keep in touch, she'd say, "What would your father say?" Every time an old landmark was razed, she would say it. And she'd say it again when a new building took its place.

After a time she used it as an admonition. When she looked one of us straight in the eye, it was more like, "Mind your *p*'s and *q*'s."

Today, though from a totally different perspective, I, too, wonder what my father would say.

His favorite radio program was "The Life of Riley." Had he lived a few years longer, my father could have watched the jocular William Bendix on a screen right in his living room. *What* would he have said to that?

To him, the only men who wore long hair were those who preferred symphonic music or sold cough drops.

He understood that "cuttin' a rug" was swinging to music, but *disco* . . . ?

He approved of WPA and CCC and NRA, but HEW, NASA, ERA, and Proposition 13 would all have been New Deals to him.

His grandchildren's trips to Europe never resulted in the telling of enchanting tales as did his annual treks to the state fair.

His salary was less than today's paycheck deductions, so I guess he would have been appalled at the current cost of a pound of steak, a gallon of gasoline, or a hair cut.

How would he have felt about his great-grandchil-

From over My Shoulder

dren – the girls in overalls, the boys using hair dryers? No one ever sang "You deserve a break today" to him, so he settled for a five-cent White Castle burger. He thought the high jinks of Fatty Arbuckle, the murder of William Desmond Taylor, and the affairs of Peaches and Daddy Browning were real scandals. But then, he never heard of the obliterated eighteen-minute tape.

What would my father have said to all of this? Plenty!

It was during one of my yearly visits with my father's parents that I was first faced with finding my own diversions. Visiting these grandparents was not the over-the-river-to-Grandmother's-house trip that you read about in storybooks. It was a five-hour journey on a scratchy, green train seat to a huge, grey stucco house. Therein lived my grandparents and five unmarried aunts and uncles.

In the parlor, where the carpet was never walked on and the furniture never sat on, was a phonograph. This was my entertainment; the phonograph and two records, one by Harry Lauder, the other by Madame Schumann-Heink. It was the latter that I played over and over. Her range – from the lowest gutteral to the highest shrill – suited my need. By letting the spring run down, then rewinding it slowly with the needle still on the record, I could produce a sound that was sidesplitting.

So many of my memories are of the good old summertime when the living was supposedly easy. Looking back, it now seems we spent most of the summer preparing for the next winter.

Storm windows had to be painted and puttied before storing. Ashes were hauled from the basement. Gardens were spaded, plowed, planted, watered, and weeded. We scarcely had time to finish picking and preserving fruits and berries when the cucumbers and tomatoes were staring at us from heaping baskets.

Even getting ready for that once-a-week day of rest was work. With the dauber in the bottle of shoe white, we cleaned our white shoes – white *canvas* shoes, with a grosgrain ribbon bow. Actually we weren't cleaning them at all, we were painting them, and, until they were thoroughly dry, they were a dark grey.

On this one day of rest, my father sometimes walked to

town and returned with a pint of vanilla ice cream. We'd all be waiting with a dish and spoon, because it was at the pouring stage by the time he reached home with it.

When the thermometer climbed, we'd turn on the hose on the west side of the house in the late afternoon. And we ran behind the ice wagon snitching pieces of ice from the sawdust. We popped the tiny splinters into our mouths and carried larger chunks home to cool our lemonade.

I think about Sunday dinners in those days, too. Sunday dinners – always so special and served at noon. Fried chicken, milk gravy, biscuits, and apple pie. Then I remember the day before in the backyard – chasing the big, brown hen, the hatchet and the tree stump, the hot water and the feathers. And I ask myself, "Was it all *that* special?"

Often on hot summer days, I recall the spot where we went swimming, a sort of millpond between a broken dam and a fallen tree. No lifeguard, no rules, no admission. Just a lot of splashing and hooligan tricks. And then I remember the bloodsuckers between our toes, the broken glass, and the rusty nails along the embankment. And I ask myself, "is there anything more inviting than the aqua splendor of a swimming pool?"

Unforgettable was the huge Wehrle kitchen range that stood on ornately carved legs in my mother's kitchen. Made of solid steel, it had six holes for cooking and a warming closet on the top. It was a massive thing. We dipped warm water from the porcelain-lined reservoir and toasted our feet in front of the open oven door. How cozy it was – in the winter. Only in the winter. Sometimes splinters of wood and coal dust fell to the floor when it was filled. The ashes were scooped from a little trap on the very bottom. "Was it all *that* cozy?"

So long ago it was – but it seems only yesterday – my mother would say, "Did anyone put out the milk bottle?" or "I must write the milkman a note to leave coffee cream."

A quart of fresh milk was delivered by the milkman each day. The milk wagon was white with Sanitary Dairy printed on the side. It was horse-drawn, and I suspect the horses' tails swishing away the flies justified the word *sanitary*.

From over My Shoulder

In the summer mother said, "Someone bring in the milk before the sun hits it." In winter, "Someone bring in the milk before it freezes." The latter was the best of all. As children, we wanted it to freeze. The cream, which was always on the top in those days, would push the little cardboard stopper four or five inches above the bottle's top. We'd bring it in and slice this creamy part. Then each of us would have a circle of "iced cream" to sink into the center of a bowl of hot oatmeal—but not until Mama had examined it to make sure the cat hadn't licked it first!

There was a time, perhaps earlier, when we bought our milk at the creamery. I always hated the smell inside that place, but I loved watching two girls cutting and wrapping pounds of butter. We brought our own containers and watched while they were being filled. We also brought along a little tin pail with a cover. This we had filled with buttermilk—for free!

When I stand in front of a dairy counter today, I think, "You've come a long way." We've long since been accustomed to pasteurized milk but how about homogenized, low-fat skim, chocolate, chocolate low-fat, eggnog, acidophilus, 2 percent skim, slender skim, cultured buttermilk, half-and-half, homo 2 percent, and Vitamin A and D enriched?

Maybe milk today *is* better, but it will never taste better than the warm, foamy stuff I drank from a tin cup in my uncle's cow barn. Now *that* was milk—right from the faucet!

Much of our shopping for food was done at our neighborhood grocery. These little markets were usually a portion of the storekeeper's home. They operated from either a lean-to adjacent to the house itself or the living room was the store and the dining room, a miniwarehouse.

The one in our neighborhood was a neat little bungalow. There were no advertising signs, but the service was tops. The meat was cut right before our very eyes, and Mr. Fox the owner would leave his dinner table to cut us "a quarter's worth of beefsteak." He'd drop the hoe right where he stood in his garden to pack us a pint of ice cream.

He offered no coupons, no trading stamps, no cash

drawings. What he did offer was the first slice of dried beef off the hand-operated meat slicer. If you had a cold, he'd give you a stick of horehound candy.

There was a case full of candy. All kinds and colors of unwrapped candy for a penny and some for two for a penny. It brought a kind of sparkle to a child's eyes that Disneyland would find hard to equal today.

Mr. Fox and his wife didn't keep "store hours." They were there in the early morning and in the late evening. And they were there when gas was rationed. We were walking in those days, toting heavy bags of food, so the neighborhood grocery was mighty handy.

Then the war ended, and we were driving our cars again and parking them in huge parking lots. Soon we were walking down long aisles, tossing packaged food into carts, and standing in long checkout lines.

The little neighborhood grocery couldn't compete. If ever anyone was justified in saying, "Where were you when I needed you?" it was the small, neighborhood grocer.

Nostalgia, I'm told, is homesickness. Somehow I can't think of it that way. I can become nostalgic about a definite time or event with no feeling of homesickness. For example, I well remember how the drain pan under the icebox would sometimes overflow, and little rivers would run across the linoleum rug, but I surely feel no homesickness over it. I've never even felt any longing for the return of a refrigerator that had to be defrosted manually. So, to me, nostalgia is looking back, but not with regret or sadness.

To some of us, remembering and reliving are the means of passing away time. To others, too young for recall of this range, there is also a certain fascination.

Call it nostalgia . . . daydreaming . . . woolgathering— whatever. There is an afterglow to moments we have known, and they should be revived. Each of us has had our special moments.

It was a wondrous place. I sat on a high stool, legs dangling, elbows leaning on a solid marble counter, and ordered a Coke. A *cherry* Coke. The soda jerk pulled a han-

From over My Shoulder

dle, and the savory refreshment fizzed over the crushed ice. With the heel of his hand, he hit another handle, which plunged just the right amount of cherry juice into it. And I watched the whole procedure in the enormous mirror behind him.

To my back, encased in glass, were trays and trays of hand-dipped candies. The big black fan overhead revolved just enough to mix the delectable chocolate aroma with the voices of townspeople who walked by the open door. *An enchanting moment.*

It was my birthday, and I was wearing a white voile dress. Beside my dinner plate were two packages wrapped in pale blue tissue paper. In one—a gold Eversharp pencil dangling from a long, but narrow, black grosgrain ribbon. Proudly I slipped it over my head and ran for the mirror. In the other—a white satin hair bow, caught up in the center with a gold clasp. *A moment of unforgettable glee.*

I sat on a pile of lumber. Beside me was a wicker basket covered with a white cloth. I was bringing my father's noon lunch to him, but I was early. I could smell the freshly cut wood, which was stacked high all about me. I was in a forest; I was a princess; I was Hansel, and I was Gretel. Only the blast of the powerful steam whistle made me aware of my factual errand. My father lifted me up onto his workbench, where I shared his basket's contents. *A moment of eternal quality.*

The circus came to town. I was up at dawn to go down to the railroad station to watch them unload. I sat on a curb and watched the parade. I kicked a stone all the way home, because I knew I must forfeit any hope of sitting under the big top to see the entire performance—until someone dropped by with four complimentary tickets. *A spellbinding moment.*

Happiness of this kind is only a step from delirium. Moments like these will never pass my way again. Never again will I know this kind of ecstasy.

Someone says, "Oh, come on now! *Never* is a long, long time."

Don't I know it!

This is not to say that I no longer have my moments, because I certainly do.

I remember the moment my husband started his search for our birth certificates. (I looked the other way.)

There was the moment when he looked up the location of the nearest Social Security office. (Again, I pulled the curtain.)

The moment he subscribed to *Modern Maturity*, I went into a decline.

And how well I remember that moment I opened my eyes on that first day of retirement.

Had anyone been watching that day, I would have appeared a little on the daffy side. I scrubbed, baked, polished, and laundered. Frantically I dashed from one chore to another, knowing that the second I stopped I would hear the ticking of the clock.

Friends who had retired earlier gave me bits of conflicting advice. Some said I should stick to a schedule, keep myself up, and throw myself into volunteer work. Others advised me to throw away the alarm clock, to let myself go, and to do what came naturally.

All of them said, "You will love it," and all of them were wrong.

I have never loved it, but I have endured it. I have not made the best of it, but I have learned from it.

I have learned never to start a sentence with, "When I was your age . . . ," "That reminds me . . . ," or "Kids in my day . . ."

From bitter experience, I have learned that I know better than anyone in this world what is, and is not, good for me.

I know that a wisp of flattery directed at me may stem from sincerity, but I am also aware that it may be the result of some kid's mother telling him to say it.

I am very sure that no one is interested in what I paid for a can of salmon in 1930, and that's one reason I mutter to myself.

The only people who would listen to me tell what rough going we had during the Great Depression are those who lived through it, and they already know.

From over My Shoulder

I was also told to keep busy. "Keeping busy is the secret," someone said.

Keeping busy is fine—all well and good, but convincing anyone that you are busy is futile. No one believes there is any way to be really busy in life after retirement. I, for one, have no intention of spelling it out for them. I know why I am busy, and if I understand it, that's all that is necessary.

First, I spend a lot of time looking for things. Sometimes I find them in the refrigerator, the silver drawer, and even in the wastebasket. Other articles just plain disappear, and I never see them again, whereas still others reappear right where I thought I had left them.

Also, each day I set aside a little quiet time for myself—a little part of each day devoted to worrying. I truly believe that the things we worry about never happen; therefore, I don't want to get behind on it.

So I don't tell anyone that I'm busy. I don't give them the chance to query, "Doing what?"

In all areas, I watch my step. I keep myself alerted to what the consequences will be should I slip up on any of them.

When you're old, you have to try harder.

The Geriatric Gap

Throughout my childhood days, growing old was a feat accomplished only by grandparents and a scattered assortment of aunts and uncles. I suppose I knew that some day my own parents would reach this time in life, but I didn't dwell on it. As for *me* ever "getting up there?" Unthinkable!

Some of my friends came from a three-generation home, their grandparents having sold the homestead. From the outside looking in, it seemed a good enough arrangement. If any of these kids resented giving up space—a room of their own—they didn't show it. Grandpa and Grandma were too old to work any longer, someone must watch out for them. That's just the way it was.

Today it is a whole new picture, and kids are a whole new breed. Are Grandma and Grandpa going to move in with *them?* Indeed not! You can bet your Medicare benefits on it. *Their* grandparents will go into something called *retirement*, and these kids know all about it.

The following excerpts were taken from letters written by ten third-grade students.

"Retirement is when someone stops his or her job. Mostly it is when that person is over sixty. When they retire people

The Geriatric Gap

like to play bingo. When I retire I will get ready for bed and say my prayers and hope not to die."

"Retirement is when you are old. You retire from your job and use money from your retirement fund to live. I would go outside and ly [sic] in my hammock when I get one and I would dream and I would watch TV. Stuff like giuding [sic] light and how the world turns."

"Retirement is when someone works and they are old and they can't work forever. Then they stay home and don't work. I would make some friends and play checkers."

"I would be bored. When or if I get retired. But if I do get retired I would invent some things."

"If I was old and I retired I would feel sad because I would not have anything to do. If I was sixty-five years old I would relax and clean up the house. I would spend my money on food or maybe a vacation. Or I would sell my house and go to a semetery [sic]."

"Retirement is . . . I don't know. If I was retired I would feel really bad and probably not talk to anyone. If your boss said you were retired you would be about seventy years old. You might move to your neighbors house or talk it over with someone or go to a bar and drink a lot."

"Retirement is when somebody gets too old for the job the person is in and then the person leaves the job. They sit around and look for a job for older people. I would go on a trip to California and maybe to New York and I would go to the Shrine circus a lot."

"Retirement is when you have a job and you have worked for the co. and you get old and retire. You quit. If I retired I would get up and drink some coffee and go to a ball game."

"Retirement is when a person is at a serten [sic] age when people are too old to work and decide to retire. People sometimes give farewell parties and they ushely [sic] retire when their sixty-three. They don't do much."

"Retirement is when someone retires from high school and then they go work at a college."

So there we have it—straight from the eight- and nine-year-olds of today. They are perceptive. They have enough insight and sophistication to make us glad they *are* different.

Half the problem in spanning the geriatric gap could be solved by simple translating.

Let's face it—slang is here to stay. If "my old lady" and "my old man" strike you as distasteful, think back on the jargon of sheiks and flappers.

Keep an open mind, swap today's lingo with your own, and you'll know "where they're coming from." When they ask, "What's happening?" you'll be ready with, "What's cooking?"

Don't feel ridiculed if you're called a "nerd" or a "turkey." Instead, snap back "So's your old man!" and everyone within earshot will know you are no "boonie."

There will be those who don't "dig" you—they won't get your "drift." They'll label you as "up tight." Calmly, in a "laid back" manner, tell them you are *not* the "wreck of the Hesperus." Then add, "Now, you savvy?"

"Alri-i-i-i-ght! That's neat!" they'll answer.

And this is where you say, "Keen!"

This rewording won't be the total answer. Too much has changed in the passage of years. For example, this joke:

"Jack's been jilted by a street cleaner's daughter."
"Why doesn't he sewer?"

Do *not* tell this joke.

In the first place, today's youth won't know what "jilted" means. And in the second place, you may be attacking a minority group in referring to street cleaners. At any rate, they are sure to tag the whole thing as "gross." "Weird," at best.

Sometimes "getting with it" is very difficult, even though you've "got plenty of smarts." But "keep your cool" and hope they'll "bounce it off you" again. If they don't, tell them to "go cook a radish." That will "blow them away."

Remembering there was a time when you were considered to be "the cat's meow" makes "being out of it" all the

The Geriatric Gap

more painful. You were the proverbial "Charlie Boy, who thrilled 'em and chilled 'em with shivers of joy." Or you were the "it girl" or the "sweetheart of Sigma Chi."

Those were the days when *we* had "our act together." This country has always been catchword-conscious. Today the art of eloquence is all but dead, not because no one has the knack to compose a flowery phrase, but because we'd rather hear it from someone else first.

I have never quite understood how certain words make it into the top ten. Words that have lain dormant for centuries somehow are brought back into use, veiled in a whole new image. Take, for example, "gross." As long as a gross was twelve dozen of something or other, it didn't have a chance. But when the intent became "sensual" or "low-minded," it became popular faster than Bo Derek's braids.

I read somewhere that if you talk funny, you should blame your ancestors. What's happening today has nothing to do with our forefathers. So unless you're running around saying, "twenty-three skiddoo," you can forget that. Today speech is trendy; people yearn to get into the act. We hear a word or an expression used in a way that is new to us, and we think, "Ah! Good word! Cute, bright, clever!" Then, because we too want to be cute, bright, and clever, we start looking for ways to use the word.

Remember when everything from an all-purpose cleaner to a hair-raising experience was "fantastic?" Once we saw the reaction, good old words like *great* and *wonderful* seemed feeble.

The next time a waitress serves me my food and says, "There you go," I think I will.

Not since someone got a laugh with the word *weird* have we heard anything dubbed as "spooky" or "mysterious."

When we can't come up with anything more vivid, we toss it off with "something else," as in "that guy is something else." People, things, and places are all "something else." Though they may be outstanding, elegant, or exotic, "something else" will cover it all. It's noncommittal, and we know the listener understands because he says it all the time, too.

In the face of misfortune, we used to straighten our

shoulders and use phrases like "pick up the pieces," "carry on," and "make a fresh start." That was yesterday. Today we must say, "I have to get on with my life." Yes, that's what we must say, because that's what everyone says.

So, whether then or now, we are pushovers for jargon, and it is one of the lesser causes of a gap between generations. There are other areas where the need to bend is far more essential.

One evening at the home of friends, we had had about an hour of good, on-top-of-it conversation when someone said, "What's all this malarky today about the 'in thing,' this always having to be 'with it.' "

"Fads, just fads," another answered. "Every generation has its own. Our grandparents had theirs."

As the chatting went on, though, not one of us could remember anything faddy or frivolous in our grandparents' lives. Their wants, we agreed, centered more on protection, preservation, and survival.

Later I recalled that in my parents' time there was a thirst for "the latest thing." Without her fur neckpiece and muff, her accordion-pleated georgette frocks, my mother would have been desolate. Without his high-buttoned spats and his celluloid collar my father could not have walked out the door with her.

During my own heyday, the four-buckle galoshes, the wraparound, oversized coat, and the two-toned moire dress were all "the rage."

What of my own children's happy days? What was the "craze" then? A rainbow of cashmere sweaters, sugar-starched crinolines, bobby sox, and saddle shoes.

Today's passion is jeans. It wouldn't be fair to call them a fad. A fad is something everyone is interested in for only a short time, and this is not true of jeans.

Jeans are forever. They are everlasting; their popularity is endless. It just goes on and on, and I do not understand it.

I'm told that they are comfortable, but they surely do not look comfortable. I'm told that they are "easy," yet when I see the wriggling it takes to get into these dandy little denims, I wonder.

The Geriatric Gap

I do concede. There must be something I don't see because almost everyone else loves them. And almost everyone wears them. That, of course, is the sad part.

One thing I do understand is their high cost. If you must run around with Vanderbilt, Calvin, or Tiegs on your backside, you're going to have to pay for it.

Jeans aren't anything new, you know. Oh, my, no! I remember when having nothing to wear *except* blue jeans was the cause of many a kid dropping out of school.

So jeans aren't a fad, and they aren't new. Jeans are the proverbial silk purse made from a sow's ear.

Something I do understand, but find hard to swallow, is the shifting of authority as one generation takes over from another.

Last September, hoping for one last swipe at summer, our entire family decided to spend a few days at the lake. It was on one of those days that I found myself the only spectator to what seemed to be a three-ring water show.

The younger ones were leaping from a raft into floating inner tubes. Their shrieks and laughter carried across the water to where I sat trying to read. They were shoving, pushing, slipping, and falling. I wanted to cry out, "Cool it, out there, before someone gets hurt!"

Far out on the lake, now only a tiny speck, two of the older ones were bobbing around in a sailboat. Peering at them through my binoculars relieved some of my uneasiness, but why, I wondered, did they have to go out so far? I wanted to shout, "Do whatever it is you must do to head that thing back here!"

Others whizzed by me on skis behind a high-powered boat. Again and again they circled the island, swung toward shore, kicked off one ski, and continued at a chilling speed. I wanted to call out to them, "That's enough for today. Come wash your hands before dinner."

I turned my attention to a young man who was hurling a stick into the water and to the brown and white spaniel retrieving it. I pushed my glasses back up into place. I opened my book and closed it again.

Once more I resigned myself to letting go. I must not stand up, wave my arms, and make demands and assertions. The upper hand now belongs to another generation. My wire-pulling days are over. I have lost control. This is not a sudden realization, because seldom does anything come to me *suddenly*. But I did recall a time when my husband and I had discussed this.

I had told him how I could see the place of authority shifting. I wanted him to be aware of my willingness to step down. I hoped he would notice the absence of apron strings and any of the other ties that bind. Admittedly there had been some reluctance, but all in all, I'd truly loosened the reins.

He said something about, "Once a dictator, always a . . . " It was a short discussion.

Again I watched the young man – still tossing the stick – the spaniel still chasing after it.

There was a second dog, older, much older, than the spaniel. She was sitting beside me. She'd been sitting close to me a lot that summer. All this activity seemed to unnerve her, so when she'd found this quiet place she had clung to it. I reached down and scratched her head. She opened her eyes, moved even closer, sighed, and settled down again.

Once she retrieved sticks. Once I jumped from a raft.

If I had any doubts about who had replaced me at the helm, they were dismissed one afternoon when I was visiting one of my daughters. I stood clutching my robe about me as she coaxed me to join her in the jacuzzi.

"Get in," she shouted, "what are you waiting for?"

"I'm waiting until no one is looking," I answered. "I'm such a sight in a swim suit."

"For heaven's sake, what do you expect at your age?"

"Well, I must say, you don't mind being blunt."

"Do you want me to lie to you?"

"A little, yes."

"Would you have believed me if I'd said you look like Jaclyn Smith?"

"No, but I'd have had fun trying."

I know I taught my children to be forthright and

The Geriatric Gap

honest, but I don't recall dwelling much on freedom of speech. They've picked that up, a lot of it, along the way.

The minute I pulled a casserole from the oven one night, I knew something was wrong with it, but I served it anyway. How could I possibly suppose *my* family would politely, and quietly, nibble away at it?

With the first taste, one of them exclaimed, "Ye gods! What's this supposed to be?"

"Chicken Divan," I answered, "but I forgot the chicken."

"You sure did. Yuck!" another cried, as one by one, they traipsed, plates in hand, toward the kitchen disposal.

"Did it ever occur to any of you that I do have feelings?" I asked.

"Surely, you don't expect us to sit here and eat that stuff just to spare your feelings."

"Must you always call everything by its right name?" I went on. "Do you think you always have the right to say what you think?"

"Of course, we do. And so do you."

Malarky! When something goes awry in the life of one of my children and I offer sympathy, I'm blowing the whole thing out of proportion. If I try to whitewash a worrisome situation, I don't realize the seriousness of it. And if ever I say, "I told you so," then nothing I can say or do for the next two months will make me the fair-haired mother again.

To say what one thinks is the right of every red-blooded American except those who are mothers of grown children.

Outside the family circle I know there is a tendency today for young people to talk down to those of us in our vintage years. I know, too, that we oldies are apt to bristle when this happens.

When a young salesclerk asked me for my telephone number one day, I couldn't think of it. Not about to reveal the self-deficiency I was suffering, I said, "You know how it is. How often does one call her own number?" Flashing me a patronizing smile, he said, "I guess when I'm your age, I won't even know my own name."

Wow! Another milestone! I've had trees fall on me

before, but not of this magnitude. (Besides, that's *my* line.)

I know a seventy-nine-year-old lady who drives from the West Coast to the Midwest once a year. She says if she gets sleepy while driving, she turns the cooler vent so air blows across her face. She sets her cruise control at 75 mph, and, when I asked her why she never gets a speeding ticket, she said, "Oh, I do. But I just consider it part of the cost of the trip." (That's like picking flowers in a park, because the $10 fine is less than the cost of a bouquet at a florist shop.) Yet I have to hand it to her, so I said, "When I'm your age, I won't know the brake from the accelerator."

There's a man who dons a red suit every Christmas Eve and plays Santa Claus to the children in his neighborhood. He's ninety-three and has been doing this for twenty-two years. To him I said, "When I reach your age, I won't know Christmas from the Fourth of July!"

I've read about an eighty-year-old lady in Florida who's out on her bicycle every morning at six o'clock, seven days a week, picking up aluminum cans for recycling. Of her I've remarked, "When I'm her age, I won't be able to bicycle *or* recycle."

I have an elderly aunt, who, at age eighty-six, can wear me to a nubbin on a shopping trip. I keep saying, "Let's stop for a cup of coffee," but she doesn't even hear me. By the time I've put her on her homeward-bound bus, I'm ready to drop—completely bushed. Every time I sigh, "*That* woman! One more jaunt like that, and I'll never *reach* her age."

Now here's this kid telling me what he'll be like when he is my age. And here am I . . . insulted, but secretly conceding that I've been guilty of the same thing a hundred times or more.

But when I say it, I'm speaking of people who are *really* old. And, like I keep trying to tell you, I'm not *really* old. When I get really old, I'll feel differently about a crack like that . . . I think.

That's the way it is for those of us who are only sort of old. On the one hand, we have those who reached the Great Plateau a few years ahead of us, and we marvel at their enduring proficiencies. On the other, there are the prime-time

The Geriatric Gap

youth. It is with them that we need to practice restraint.

But when we do relate happenings of long ago to those still in their springtime years, it is done for two reasons: To enlighten them on the hardships we endured and the pitfalls we avoided; and to brief them on the merits of our time – the simple pleasures, the sheer joy of living each sin-free day.

Whatever our avowed aim, our true aim is to impress them in a way that is to our advantage. Unfortunately this is not always the result. Sometimes they quip, "You made that up!" Disbelief – candid and aboveboard – and who can blame them? Looking back I sometimes doubt the accuracy of my own recall.

One example in particular is the dance marathon. How can anyone describe those men and women dragging each other around for seven and eight days in a maniacal competition? No less zany, though, were those of us who drove miles and paid money to watch them.

Another thing – did our parents really put their cars up for winter? I mean, did they really store it in the garage all winter long . . . up on blocks . . . drained of every last drop of whatever . . . covered with a blanket?

And what in heaven's name was that translucent slime that my grandmother used for preserving eggs? She kept them in a big crock on the top step under the cellar door. Running my arm down through that clammy gook to retrieve those eggs was one of the most terrifying experiences of my childhood.

No wonder our offspring sometimes think we are concocting tall tales.

Convincing them that they live in a time and place where the living is easy is a losing argument. For every story we tell of innocence unlimited, they can match it with one about peer pressure. Forget the hard times saga. They've got taxes like we never dreamed of.

It is far easier to point out what was good in the old days. Picture for them the kettle of beans and ham hocks bubbling on the back of the old cookstove. Let them compare that to anything slammed in and out of a microwave.

24

Tell them about the yellow Studebaker you bought for $840 and how anyone with 35¢ in his pocket could obtain a driver's license.

Now you've got their attention. There's no denying that those really were the days. This is the place to stop.

Save the flagpole sitters, the fish you caught with a piece of string, and the blizzard of '36 for another time.

There's a limit to how much they can swallow.

Himself

My neighbor Edna says men are all alike. She can't really mean it. She must remember, as I do, a time when men came in a fine and varied assortment. Each had his own peerless qualities. It is only because they have been tossed into the same boat that they *seem* to be alike. And what culprit is responsible for this? The years—the passing of the years.

Once the aging process is underway, there is a hankering to hash over long-ago happenings. There were the good times, the bad times, the sad times or glad times. But all of them *old* times and worthy of recapturing.

Because men are less reluctant to relate anything that might reveal their age, gathering together for an exchange of remember whens is a pastime more popular with them than with women. One's recollections are prodded by those of another. A certain hunger is satisfied in a hearty, healthy, and often humorous way.

In retrospect, yesterday does seem more acceptable than today, but these gents aren't looking for a place to lay the blame. Though they have long since given up on changing the face of the world, they aren't making a total mental retreat.

For a long time they've known how fast times flies. Now they're aware that the older you get, the *faster* it flies. They look back on the days when the going wage was a dollar a day, and the day was from dawn to dusk. How well they remember the blizzards of '36. There were floods and dust storms, too—in what year did they happen?

They recount in detail that time in fourth grade when old Bernard Haverill got flogged with the rubber hose. Whatever happened to "old Barney?"

They josh each other. "I'll never forget the night you fought that bear at the carnival." And "How about the day you traded your violin for that horse?" They chortle. They chuckle. They tell stories that they say folks today wouldn't believe.

They are not *living* in the past. It's just that, now and then, they enjoy wandering to this hill, ". . . to watch the scene below."

"How can you fellows continue to find something to talk about?" I asked my husband, Martin, one day.

"We'll never run out. Know why? Because we all know what we're talking about, that's why."

"You mean you all have the same opinions?"

"Right! We've seen it all. We know what's going on today and we know what the outcome will be."

"Then you are all alike?"

"Pretty much so."

"That does it!" I cried. "I all but lost one of my very best friends defending you *and* your friends on that score. She said you were all alike, and I said that wasn't true; that each of you had your own sterling traits . . . that you were individuals."

"True, true," he went on. "We have all that *plus* the insight it takes to be successful."

"This is getting sickening. I don't want to hear any more."

"You never could tell when I was joking, could you?"

He is right. I never could.

Maybe we were in too big a hurry to get married, but

Himself

after we'd dated for four years, been engaged for two, and met parents, grandparents, sisters, brothers, and cousins on both sides, we thought we really knew each other.

The depression was nearly over and we were as ready for a new deal as was the rest of our generation. All we needed to prove was that two could live as cheaply as one. We didn't mind that the bathroom of our first apartment was down the hall. We overlooked the paper draperies and the bare threads in the rugs. The sofa's exposed springs we covered with a folded army blanket.

Martin's daily wage was $6.32, and we got by. We not only got by, we saved $5.00 each month toward the $300 we would need for a down payment on a home of our own. If it wasn't the best of beginnings, neither was it the worst.

Together we raised a family. Together we rejoiced, grieved, and dreamed. We shared both the joys and the burdens. And we battled—the world and each other. But we have never—*never* in forty-six years—laughed together. Separately yes, but never at the same time.

One time, while driving along the highway, he said, "Sure is cloudy, but the weatherman said no participation." Then he roared with laughter while I sat there trying to figure it out.

"Joke! It's a *joke!* I said *participation* instead of *precipitation*. You don't get it? Anyone except you would know I did it purposely."

"Let's hope so," I answered.

Another time I read aloud from the *Reader's Digest*. "A man ran up to the ticket window just as the commuter train pulled out. 'That's my train,' he panted to the clerk. 'If I run, can I catch it?' 'Mister,' said the clerk, 'if you run, you can *beat* it.' " I thought this was a riot. By the time I'd finished reading it, I was howling.

"Always the railroads," my husband replied. "If the government would do half for the railroads that they've done for . . ."

"Oh, for heaven's sake," I interrupted. "It wasn't meant to bad mouth the railroads!"

"It wasn't? Read that over. If that's not a slam at the railroad's service . . ."

Martin also has a little phrase he employs in almost any situation. He uses it to pass the buck, to get himself off the hook, to cover his chagrin, and sometimes just because he thinks it's funny. It's not. It is brief, concise, and stupid, but it isn't funny.

I suppose you could call it a form of self-defense. Whereas some men use karate and judo, Martin has his five little words: "You know how women are!"

When our children were small, one of them took a bad tumble on the school playground. When she came home, I questioned her as to where it hurt, applied the much-adored Band-Aids, and assured her that she was okay. When her father came home, she limped out to meet him. "Stand up straight!" he shouted. "How long has one of her shoulders been lower than the other!"

"Ever since she saw you drive in," I answered.

"I'm calling the doctor!"

After describing the accident, he absolved his own fran-

Himself

tic behavior with, "I doubt it's anything serious, Doc. But if you'd take a look at her, I know her mother would feel better. You know how women are."

Seeing this work for him over a long period of years has become tiresome and revolting.

There was the time he thought he smelled gas in the house and called the utility company. As the serviceman was leaving, he said, "Thanks for coming out. My wife wouldn't have slept a wink tonight if I hadn't had it checked out. You know how women are!"

On a stormy day a few months ago, we *agreed* it would be foolhardy for a couple our age to drive in inclement weather just to keep a dinner date. When he called with our regrets, he couldn't resist those famous last words. "I've driven in worse weather. If it were just me, it would be different, but you know how women are."

When he turned from the phone, I said, "I heard you talking to Doug. Did he know how women are?"

"I guess he did. He sure did laugh."

"Doug has been a loyal and dependable friend all through the years. Somehow, for me, the punch has gone out of that."

"What the heck . . . it's only an expression."

"No, it's more than that. It's an implication. There's an overtone there that says women are all alike, and this isn't true. You can go out right now and ask every woman you meet—they'll all tell you the same thing."

In all fairness, I must say that Martin does not consider himself a lampshade-on-the-head clown. And that's good because he definitely isn't.

He refers to himself as an optimist. I think of him as someone who is forever trying to cheer me up when I don't want to cheer up.

Sitting here in this closet—just me, my typewriter, and a sheet of blank paper—isn't exactly what I'd planned for my golden years, but that's the way it is.

To Martin, a silent typewriter is louder than a clicking one, so quite often, I write, "How now, brown cow. Every good boy does fine. abcdefghijklmnopqrstuvwxyz and ABCDEFGHIJKLMNOPQRSTUVWXYZ." And sometimes, "!#$%¢()_+." One day I couldn't make even this small effort, and sure enough, from the far end of the house, I heard, "Stuck for something to write about?"

"Something will come to me," I chirped in a light voice.

"Why don't you tell 'um about the time you went to that wedding where the photographer followed you throughout the reception, taking pictures of you. Wonder if he ever developed that one he took from the back when you were leaning over the guest book. You were all gussied up and thought he was taking your picture for the society page. Come to find out he had mistaken you for the groom's mother. That really ruffled your feathers because you were only eleven years older than the groom. Why don't you tell 'um about that?"

"Or how about the time you ran across that old memory book. You said, 'Oh, look—that was the year that instead of dotting my *i*'s, I was making circles over them.' So then I said, 'Now you've got circles *under* your eyes.' Remember that?"

"I remember."

"Have you ever told them about that day . . . ?"

"Oh, I'm sure I have."

"Did you get all that down?"

"Word for word."

"Need any more?"

Actually I didn't need that much.

Few things have puzzled me quite like, "Why do two people, shuffling about in the same house year after year (after year), waste time *arguing*?" I put the question before a few of my peers over coffee one morning.

The answers ranged from boredom to becoming crotchety and solved nothing. On three points we all agreed: (1) we did have verbal, and sometimes loud, disputes; (2) the topic could be anything or nothing; (3) the arguments started with no motivation, no provocation, and no warning. But why?

In desperation I turned to Holly Meeker. Dear little Holly. In all the years I'd known her, I'd never heard her state her name with any real conviction. Yet unlike the rest of us, when she did come up with something—it was something.

Himself

She started slowly and gained momentum as, one by one, we started leaning toward her. "It has to do with honesty. It's like when you stub your toe and the phone rings at the same time. You grab the receiver and *scream* yes, not because you're angry with the person calling, but because your toe hurts. But the person calling doesn't know that."

"Go on, Holly," I prompted, "where does the honesty come in?"

"Well, if you're honest, you'll admit that you're irritated because you stubbed your toe, even though you lashed out at the person nearest you. See?"

We saw.

I saw – but I was slow to tumble. One night Martin and I were watching Jimmy Stewart on the "Tonight" show. Martin was holding a magazine in front of his face, but I was on the edge of my chair.

I said, "Sh–h–h! I don't want to miss a word he says."

"A word he stammers would be more like it."

"That's his forte. I l–o–v–e it!"

"You wanta know something I'd love? I'd love to have some buttons on those two shirts hanging on the doorknob in there."

Sometimes these things take time. About a week later, Martin sauntered out in the kitchen where I had forty things going, and said, "I've been watching that old *Kitty Foyle* movie again. That Ginger Rogers – she had it all. And I guess she's still got it, because she's got a nightclub act right today, and she looks p–r–e–t–t–y darn good."

"Sure, with twenty college kids holding her up, three inches of makeup, and a blonde wig. I see you've dripped coffee grounds again . . . and when are you going to empty the wastebaskets?"

"Hey! If you want the wastebaskets emptied, just say so. But don't attack me just because you think you look twenty years older than Ginger Rogers."

I wondered if he'd been talking to Holly Meeker. Or does it really take one to know one? This, I wanted to believe. For days I found myself humming "Getting to Know You."

I'd heard that people who live together for many, many

years start thinking alike, and sometimes even looking alike. I was beginning to agree with this.

I was noticing that many times Martin would bring up a subject that happened to be the very thing I too was thinking about. Often an unfinished sentence was left hanging in the air, yet we both knew how it would have ended—had it ended. For a time our conversations seemed to flow like wine. Then it happened. It was a Tuesday, sometime after noon, and I asked a question. That's where I went wrong.

"Why," I asked, "why, *why* can you not give me a reasonable answer—ever?"

"Because you ask silly questions."

"That's stupid," I told him. "It's just another cop-out. My questions are not silly."

"When you ask me what time it is and you've got a watch on your own wrist, I call that silly."

"Oh, that! If you remember, I was in the basement, my watch had stopped, and I was timing something in the oven. So your answer, 'time for the news,' wasn't much help."

Before he could pick up on the belabored story of how I never wind my watch, I moved on to the next gripe, which I'd been harboring for months.

We were sidling our way down the aisle of a plane. My overnight case was banging my varicose veins with every step. I kept bumping my head on the storage bins each time I leaned over to peer at the seat numbers. There were people ahead of me trying to back up and people behind me trying to pass. And behind those people was Martin. With all the humility and innocence any human being could muster, I quaked, "What are our seat numbers?"

You won't believe his answer. "Just keep going."

Having unloaded all this, having refreshed his memory on each tiny detail, I said, "That was degrading. I'll bet half the people on that plane thought I couldn't read!"

"Oh, they did," he cracked. "Didn't you hear them? All the way to Denver, they kept saying, 'See that lady over there? She can't read.' "

I was willing to let him have this last word, but only because I thought I had gotten my point across. Will I ever learn? The very next day, after we'd eaten only a sandwich for lunch, I said, "Would you like a dish of peaches?"

Himself

His answer? "No, I had a dill pickle."
I didn't get it—but neither did I question it.
Many are the times that he doesn't get me either. Why I am the way I am is something I can't explain, so I'm happy that he doesn't ask for reasons. He makes a list of my peculiarities, and he recites them to me, but he's not interested in excuses. This is good, because everything I do is done innocently.

For example, never in all our years together have I ever felt I wanted to hit him in the head, so when I tossed a pair of tennis shoes down the clothes chute that time, I never dreamed he'd be standing directly beneath the opening in the basement.

I heard him shout, "What the . . . !"; and the next thing I knew he was coming up the steps holding his head.

"You know, if you want to get rid of me, you've come up with the perfect plan. No judge in the world would ever believe it. It would be case dismissed, and you'd get off scot-free."

I said, "I'm sorry," and tried not to laugh.

"You amaze me, you really do. With timing like that, you could put Bob Hope out of business. With aim like that, you could bag a five-pointer with a K-Mart bow and arrow. Yet somehow you can't feed a thread through a needle to sew a shirt button on for me. You are totally inconsistent."

"I'm a streetcar named *Denial*. Right?"

"Something like that," he said, still rubbing his head.

I've heard it a hundred times, but he chooses to outline it all for me again.

There was the time in San Francisco when I left our motel at 11:00 P.M. to take a walk, but the next day I jumped up on the dresser when I saw a mouse.

He reminds me of the time I had a broken ankle set without making a peep and then of the time I became nauseous when he removed a sliver from my finger.

It seems I shove furniture from one wall to another, but call him to the kitchen to open a jar of marmalade. He can't grasp this situation at all.

"You've known me for fifty years," he says, "yet when I'm driving the car, you never take your eyes off the road. At the same time, you'll get on a plane and sleep without knowing who the pilot is—or *if* he is." (He's duped on this one. I am not sleeping; I *always* close my eyes when I'm praying.)

However, for the most part, he is right. I remember when I used to say I was going to marry a man with black, patent-leather hair—*lots* of hair! And rich—*very* rich. And understanding. Instead I married Martin.

In the early years of our marriage, there was never a

Himself

question of who got up first in the morning. In those days no one talked about day people and night people. Daylight peaked through the curtains, there was a day's work to be done, and we got up and did it. It was only after we retired from our life's work that the truth came out. Martin really was a day person. Basically I am a night person.

I have said it before, and now I repeat, "I see no reason for anyone to whistle before noon or after age sixty."

By the time my blinking eyes have guided me from the bedroom to the bathroom to the kitchen each morning, Martin is already at the table, shaved, showered, and dressed. From behind his newspaper, he chants, "There she goes—Miss America!"

It is over our third cup of the morning that we have our meaningful conversations. Always it starts with a question—his question, of course.

"Whadda ya think happened 203 years ago today?"

"The chocolate chip was discovered."

"Come to! Exactly 203 years ago on this day, George Washington's army went into winter quarters at Valley Forge."

"Imagine that!"

"Says here that nothing ever rusts in Egypt. They have cars that are fifty years old and still running like a top."

"That's nice."

"Do you know that this sunshine streaming in right here left the surface of the sun only eight minutes ago?"

"You read too many newspaper fillers."

"And you've got your glasses on upside-down."

Do I sometimes resolve that I will change my frowzy and bedraggled morning image? Heavens, no! I could never deny this man his one glorious moment. The pattern becomes him. Changing the sequence of these daily incidents would ruin his whole day.

I know. I tried it once. One morning I managed to slip out of bed, do a hasty makeup job, and start the coffee before he appeared in the kitchen. I had turned up the thermostat, brought in the paper, and put out the place mats.

He was a man betrayed. He had been demoted. He walked to the window, back to his chair; picked up his newspaper, set it aside again. He was confused—as frustrated as Rodney Dangerfield without a necktie.

Never again. Men don't like to take a back seat. Husbands don't like wives who lord it over them. So why do it? Why deprive him of this one thing he loves to gloat over?

So this is the reason I sleep late. This is the reason I lie there until I smell the coffee. It's the least I can do for him.

There are a lot of theories on why and how some marriages are long lasting.

Some say it's all give and take; others say it's keeping an open line. Many give credit to the Golden Rule, and there are those who claim an attitude of live and let live is the key.

I suspect there are as many concepts as there are aging married couples. With my husband and me, it is secrets. Yes, Martin and I have secrets.

You will understand better when I tell you about the time I mailed my lower dentures back to the dentist with a note that said start over. How did I know that the day after he'd socked that little monster into my mouth, he had cashed my check and gone to Europe? Or that anyone could be so efficient as to include that little box in his forwarded mail? As a result I ate baby food while my lowers followed him through five foreign countries.

Martin carried on for weeks. Long after he'd stopped guffawing, I'd catch him stifling a chuckle. How he would have loved to tell that one to his cronies! I was not threatened because he knows I have never divulged the happenings of one evening way back in the '50s.

Bill Haley was appearing in his Rock-Around-the-Clock concert in our city, and our teenage daughter asked if she could see him. Her father said he'd think about it. After she left the room he asked me, "What do we know about this Haley kid? Where does he live?"

Never before or since have I seen him more docile than he was when he realized his mistake. He begged, "Promise me—*promise me*—you'll never tell the kids." I never have, although I've held it over his head a time or two.

Both of us remember the time I mistook overgrown lettuce for Swiss chard and boiled it into nothingness. Neither of us will ever forget my kissing a stranger as he alighted

Himself

from the train, thinking he was Uncle John.

If I would let him, Martin would like to forget the afternoon reception we attended and the lady at the serving table who handed him a coffee cup on a saucer. He insisted on taking the saucer with the cup, and the lady was just as unyielding. He all but pulled that poor woman out of her chair before he tumbled.

The reason why our marriage has held together can be found on the back stairs of our house. You might say our marriage is built on inside information. You might call it blackmail. Whatever, it is the one area in which we have mutual understanding.

But, seriously, who reassures you when you are worried, laughs at you when you are angered, tolerates you when you're intolerable? Who pretends he understands your every emotion when he hasn't a clue?

Who runs to the market for the curry powder and again for the tomato paste, which you had forgotten? Who makes a mad dash to the post office with *your* mail? Who comes to your rescue when you've locked the keys in the car, when you've overestimated yourself and time is running out before dinner guests arrive and you can't open a jar of mayonnaise and you've dropped a raw egg on the kitchen floor? When there's a knock at the door, and you're still at the breakfast table in your jaded housecoat, who greets the visitor and holds her at bay until you've made yourself reasonably presentable?

Once I read, "When I retired, I found I had not enough money and too much husband." And there is a cross-stitch sampler that reads, "Staying out of my kitchen may prevent a few wars." Amusing, yes. But fair?

Consider a man who, for so long, has been vital, able, stouthearted, and strapping. Then comes the time when his life's circumstances have changed. All the little particulars that once constituted his day-to-day being are no longer essential. There is little, if anything, that he actually needs to do. But he's waging a fine battle. With all the bravado he can muster, he is carrying on. It is about this time—a time when he is giving a great show of stamina and might—that we choose to call his bluff and cause him to feel that he is in the way.

Let's slide out from under our halos and take another look at him. What the years have cost him is there for one and all to see. He has no makeup to conceal the facial lines and the furrowed brow, no ruffles to hide the scrawniness of his neck. There's no fabrication. No sham. He could, if he became desperate enough, stoop to a touch of Grecian Formula, otherwise what you see is what you get, and what you get is worthy of some discernment.

He still gets up early in the morning. His coffee is ready, not because he has a bustling little wife, but because he sets it with a timer the night before.

He reads three newspapers and grumbles because the TV news is the same at ten o'clock as it was at six o'clock – as it was at noon.

At least once a day, he says, "I think I'll take a walk. Stretch my legs a little."

His shoulders droop a little, but when a young girl tells him he looks younger than her father, he can button his suit coat and assume the stance of a Buckingham guard.

He's suspicious of any man his age who has a full head of hair. (It's a wig, and who does he think he's fooling?)

He doesn't take naps, but he rests his eyes a couple times a day.

He transfers a little sum from one bank to another and comes home with a digital clock or a teflon-lined pan.

He'd take his grandsons fishing more often if they'd learn to sit still for five minutes.

The company where he worked is going under. Anybody with half an eye could have seen it coming.

He hates compact cars and has been known to kick a computer.

He sits in his big chair with his only granddaughter beside him. She talks a lot. She's a reflection of another little girl he knew many years ago. He wipes his eyes.

He'll tell you that he flips his contact lenses in and out like a teenager. This doing what you darn well please, by golly, you can't beat it. He feels great – not a day older than he felt twenty years ago.

The truth isn't always in him, but you love him anyway.

Related Subjects

Enthusiasm for the family reunion runs hot and cold, depending on one's age bracket. If you're one of the small-fry, it's all fun and frolic. Later comes the gawky age when you are so shy that it's nearly day's end before you've become reacquainted with your own cousins.

Sometime during the next few years, you gain poise and bring a guest—the boy of your dreams. Your aunts and uncles assume he is your "intended" and say he seems nice enough.

Then come the years of real self-assurance. You arrive with a "covered dish," a well-established husband (not the intended, but still nice enough), two fine-looking kids, and an inflated ego.

A few more summers pass, and you're there again with the same covered dish, the same husband and *one* kid. (Wild horses couldn't drag the older one along.)

Next is a period that requires a bit of doing. The day before the family reunion, you have your hair touched up, and the nice-enough young man isn't so young anymore, and he agrees to attend another of what he calls these "ridiculous functions" only after you've stooped to blackmail. You're prepared to make excuses for your childrens' absence by explaining that they are hundreds of miles away, but you know in your heart of hearts they wouldn't have come along if they'd been in the backyard. So you walk in with your covered dish and a frozen smile.

So that's about it. From then on the young matrons are telling you that you needn't bring food. Are they sick of your covered dish? You sit there and watch the sack races and the volleyball game. You watch them return to the tables of food for second and third helpings. And you listen to the conversation.

Kevin will have his master's degree by the end of the summer. Marty has his choice of any number of scholarships. Ruthie is in her senior year at the U and is engaged to a Ph. D. No, Donald isn't just an accountant, he's a CPA. And right! Lorna isn't just a nurse; she's the head surgical nurse.

Ye gods! Doesn't anyone remember Helen Morgan crooning "My Bill?" You remember her Bill. He was just an ordinary guy.

Somewhere among us there must be at least one ordinary guy. But I, too, must confess to an unwillingness to be commonplace. I have compared and considered all things relative only to find that my one claim to a place even one notch above ordinary in this family, is the fact that I was the first child born to my parents. And I was my paternal grandparents' first grandchild *and* the first niece of several unmarried aunts and uncles.

This was a heady status, which would afford me a lifetime of undeniable rights and advantages, or so I thought.

SISTERS

Because there was no one to hand them down, my clothes were never secondhand. For the same reason my toys were new, untouched and untried.

I had no competition. My room, my desk, my books, my dolls, and even my parents were all mine, and I shared them with no one. I did not divvy so much as a stick of licorice.

For eight years, or until the first sibling was born, I maintained this standing. Though this event caused my footing to become a little less steady, it wasn't until the second sister arrived that my toehold was really weakened. Yet I yielded very little. Even then there was no contest.

Always there was the question of who "got to." Who got to go shopping in the city with Mother? Who got to sit in the front when we acquired our first car? Who got to wear lipstick? Who got to sit up late and watch the grown-ups play cards? And who got to have her own room while the other children doubled up? Who? I did. I had precedence because I had been born first.

When our parents were away, I enforced the house rules and made up a few of my own. How supremely I reigned! For such a long time I sat comfortably on that throne. Today I would be most happy to abdicate.

All the advantages and privileges have been destroyed with the passing of the years. There is no advantage in being the oldest sister, the oldest aunt, or the oldest *anything*. I question the "honor" of being the "oldest living member." When I am offered the most comfortable chair in the room, I do not feel privileged.

Sure, I may still defend my seniority, but for what? I can no longer find a way to capitalize on the favors that are available to me.

When I got to retire, got to be a grandmother, got to wear bifocals long before the others, there were no rewards. It was then I knew the old "got to game" had backfired on me, and that being first is not always best.

In spite of this, or maybe because they were never really overawed, my sisters and I have shared a togetherness that would make Lillian and Dorothy Gish look like archenemies. We have defended one another even when there was no need for it. In time of trouble, we've dropped everything to be at our sister's side.

We've cried together. Laughed at the rain together. Strolled down the lane together. And we thought it would never end, but it almost did—with a garage sale.

Why is it that the very word *sale* turns an otherwise stable and gentle woman into a shrew? It had seemed like a good idea. We all had junk to get rid of. You know—stuff that's too bad to save, yet too good to throw away. Why not pool our trash, take in the cash, subtract any expense, and divide it by three?

It started the night before the sale at my house, where the big event was to take place. I was in the garage sorting my merchandise when they drove in with their wares.

As they unpacked, the first item I saw was a set of glass luncheon trays. "Are you selling those?" I asked. "I gave them to you. If you didn't like them, you should have told me."

"Since I never use them, why should I have them cluttering my cupboards? But if that's the way you feel about it—here, take them back." So I did.

That's the way it went with item after item. We had words over a plate that had belonged to our mother. I bought a nut chopper for 25¢ and sold a towel rack for 25¢.

We took turns saying, "Why do you want to sell that?"

"It doesn't work right."

"Well, it's better than mine. I'll take this one and put mine out, and you can have whatever you can get for it."

"That doesn't seem quite fair. Give me 15¢ and it's a deal."

"I'll give you two begonias for that head scarf."

"Pots included?"

So we ended the day with a lot of stuff that was too bad to keep but too good to throw away. Before that deadly word *sale* came between us, we were giving each other things.

As I poured coffee for us, I said, "Don't forget to pay me for your share of the ad. It was $4.50, *plus tax*."

Then we laughed—all three of us . . . together.

DAUGHTERS

I'll never forget the Winter of My Disbelief. It started the eleventh day of November with a cold rain, which

Related Subjects 43

turned to sleet, which turned to snow. And it was well into April before there was any noticeable slackening in the winter's intensity. As if that weren't enough, we had a weatherman who ended every report with "and no relief in sight."

But that's not all. We also had a five-year-old, who refused to wear her boots. Well, she didn't exactly refuse, because she did put them on every morning. But somewhere between home and school, she took them off and carried them. She also carried them to within one block of home on her return from school. There she sat on the curb and pulled them on over her soggy, brown loafers. No amount of punishing, threatening, coaxing, or cajoling ever helped.

The first really warm summer day and her birthday arrived simultaneously. Dressed in a pastel organdy dress under a white eyelet-embroidered pinafore, she awaited her party guests. It wasn't until she went out to greet the firstcomers that I saw she was wearing the old rubber boots over her patent leather Mary Janes!

Throughout the games, the gift opening, the cake and ice cream, she wore the boots. When her grandparents arrived that evening, she was still wearing them.

"How come that kid's clomping around in those things on a day like this? Is it some kind of a game or something?" her grandfather asked.

"No," I said. "It's not a game—or, if it is, it's one of her own. I just could not get them off of her."

"What do you mean, you couldn't get them off of her?"

"Dad, I mean it simply is not worth the effort. She'd throw a tantrum, and then we'd both be all upset."

He didn't understand this at all. I did. I was having one of my more mellow days, but rarely am I such a softie.

My children know who is mother and who is child. I didn't wear that polka-dot "blimp" for eight and one-half months because I needed another friend. Children, too, feel this way.

Any child-rearing expert will tell you that children do not want their parents to relate to them as friends. They have friends. What they need and want are parents—a mother and a father. And from that mother and father, they want guidance, discipline, rules, leadership, and, yes, even punishment, where and when it is justified. When I first became aware of these facts, I was glad, because our children got all those things.

However, today, having reached the stage of adulthood themselves, they tell me that I overdid it. And they back this up with some pretty wild recollections.

They insist I made them hop off their bicycles and wheel through busy intersections, while their friends sailed through unscathed. They say I sent them off to music lessons before daylight on cold, blustery winter mornings. And that they'll never forget the summer I cancelled their reservations at a camp because of a polio epidemic.

It seems I forbade them to bleach one big lock of hair or to waterski until I'd had a personal interview with the driver of the boat, and they insist they never left on a date without my whispering, "Don't let the stars get in your eyes." I don't remember any of this.

What I do remember is that these children of mine were always first in everything. They were first to say, "Let's all go over to our house." When a teacher or the leader of any group asked for volunteers, they were first with an arm in the air. Whether the need was a chocolate cake, a mother to chaperone, or someone to make costumes, my children were right in there, obliging.

Most of all I remember tense hours waiting for X rays to be read. (*Which bone was it this time?*)

So today, when I see my grandchildren perched on a high limb or making their first ski jumps or lying on a gym floor with the wind knocked out of them or whizzing by on a snowmobile, I do so want to say to my children, "Now you know!"

When a grandchild is too long surfacing after a high dive, it's easy for me to unerstand why his mother starts swimming in that direction. And one night after one was in bed, he shouted, "I forgot to tell you I have to take fifteen cupcakes to school in the morning," and I smiled. But the day he traded his tennis racket for four Star War cards, I laughed out loud.

Related Subjects

Full circle – and nothing is more fulfilling.

Sitting in the bleachers and watching your grown-up kids make their own mistakes isn't easy. Resisting the temptation to say I told you so calls for a bridle and clenched teeth. So what, then, is the answer? Listening. Listening for a very long time before making any comment. Even then, let it be premeditated and short.

I do a lot of listening when our son-in-law stops in. His travels occasionally take him through our part of the country. We welcome this rare chance to hear firsthand reports on our grandchildren – their current interests and activities. It also provides a singular chance for him to air his grievances.

He tells us that the last time he was on such a trip that his wife packed up the children and moved to a motel when she saw a mouse in the laundry room.

To further point out her foolhardy inconsistencies, he says she plugs and unplugs electrical appliances with wet hands.

He would have us believe that she does not own a cookbook. Her recipe file, he claims, is an alphabetical record of the addresses and telephone numbers of the nearest McDonalds, pancake house, Shakey's Pizza, Kentucky Fried Chicken, and deli. Lately she's been talking to contractors about her dream house, which will have twelve rooms, none of them a kitchen.

One morning, pressed for time, he donned a navy suit and hurriedly pulled on a pair of brown socks. He swears he had not yet tied his shoes, when his wife shouted from the floor below, "Don't wear those brown socks with that navy suit."

At this point, he turns to his father-in-law for a word of understanding. No word is forthcoming, but they exchange "like-mother-like-daughter" glances.

Then he asks if we have ever noticed how many love seats they have in their home. The answer is four. Four love seats and not one sofa that will accommodate his 6′3″ frame.

He tells us how she avoids sad movies. She considers the evening she tearfully watched *The Way We Were* an absolute waste of time. Yet at regular intervals, she makes a point of hauling out all the letters the kids have written from camp. She reads and sobs. Reads some more and sobs some more.

I tell myself this letting off steam to us is normal. When one is stuck with faulty merchandise, one *should* go straight to the manufacturer. Here is where he can make known the imperfections with well-placed confidence.

So I offer to make amends. I tell him that he may return her, that even though eighteen years is a lengthy warranty, we will be happy to have her back any old time.

"No," he replies. "A deal is a deal."

My grandfather always said, "They mean well." After he'd given someone a dig, had said something he sort of regretted, he'd say that. And sometimes when he could think of no better way to end a conversation, he'd shrug his shoulders and say, "They mean well."

So it is with our children. They mean well. They want to be helpful in any way they can . . . to the utmost and, sometimes, to the limit.

One day our daughters called to tell us they were planning a "little something" in observance of our forty-fifth wedding anniversary. We said that would be nice.

Later they decided a "little party" would be nicer. The next time we talked, the "little party" had all the aspects of a celebration.

With my usual negative approach, I protested with "People are bored with receptions. It puts one's friends under obligation." Then I came up with the real zinger: "The whole house would need a thorough cleaning!"

They came back with "But how about Daddy? He'd just *love* it."

I said, "But *Daddy* doesn't do windows."

As it turned out, Daddy did do windows. And Daddy met planes. And everyone came home days before the big event. How many days before isn't important. For me it was only a blend of time.

For the others it was different. They had long lists of lists. Each morning they checked them with "Today we do the cream cheese and black olive thing, so this must be Tuesday."

Related Subjects

Flowers were bought, begged, and snitched. Cakes were ordered. They made sandwiches. The phone rang. Appointments were made, cancelled, and rescheduled. The lawn was mowed, raked, and clipped, after which Martin decided to trim the evergreens.

Welcome notes came from the printer with the wrong date, wet towels piled up while we waited for the washer repairman. The little people came in from the pool each afternoon—some tan, some burned, and some freckled, but all of them starving. The sandwich making was on schedule, and the phone continued to ring.

At regular intervals throughout each day, I went into my bedroom and closed the door and repeated the Serenity Prayer. Martin never missed. Each time he'd stick his head in and ask, "You all right?" So then I'd reappear back where the action was—the sandwich making and the ringing phone.

One night the California kids told the Minnesota kids all about earthquakes, and the Minnesota kids rebutted with their tornado experiences. As a result the youngest child and his grandmother had trouble falling asleep.

Finally, the big day. Although the phone still rang, the sandwiches were finished. Hair blowers were turned off, plastic garment bags were ripped from their hangers, the last dab of nail polish was applied, a broken earring was quickly mended, the bathroom and kitchen got a swipe with a paper towel, and finally, our daughters stopped asking, "How come you never bought a dishwasher?"

And so our forty-fifth wedding anniversary was *observed.*

GRANDCHILDREN

I know there are women who do not look forward to becoming a grandmother. They think it's nice, it's natural, and quite inevitable, but remain collected. They say, "Oh, yes, the baby came right on schedule. No problems. No, we haven't seen her—maybe at Christmas time."

These are the sane ones.

The rest of us, though well balanced in other areas,

regress to a state bordering lunacy when we get the word.

When my daughter said, "Mother, I'm about ten days pregnant," I screamed, "For heaven's sake why haven't you told me?"

Usually you can predict the way you will react to becoming a grandmother by the way you handled your own first-born.

After our first child was born, I assumed that everyone who came to our door—meter reader to census taker—hungered for a peek at that pink and white bit of humanity. I became a camera fiend. Whether I was sitting atop a chest of drawers, lying on the floor, or peeking around the corner, the effort to get that perfect shot was never too great.

I checked her breathing at bedtime, again in the morning, and twice during the night. When she cut a tooth, I called the pediatrician. When she laughed aloud, I called my mother. And when she took her first steps, I called her father home from work.

So, many years later when I answered my telephone and heard "Good morning, *Grandma*," it isn't surprising that I responded as I did.

I never left the telephone until I'd shared these glad tidings with everyone who cared—and some who didn't give a darn. While I feverishly flung clothes into a suitcase, I shouted at Martin to back the car out of the garage. I turned on the shower, pulled my blouse over my head without unbuttoning it, and called my office, demanding a leave of absence. Between us and this nothing-short-of-a-miracle were 200 miles. We drove them with only one stop—to buy a football and helmet.

I wish I could tell you that I improved as, one by one, the other grandchildren were born. But I didn't. Each time was just as special. It never became a middling experience, and neither have their annual visits with us.

On earlier visits, a walk to the park, a turn on the swings, and a few zips down the slides would take care of an entire morning. In the afternoons, I saw to it that they took long naps. Long, very long, naps.

Then last summer we noticed a change. The swings didn't fly as high, the slides had fewer steps, and the

Related Subjects 49

youngest one no longer took a nap. Consequently, I missed *my* forty winks.

They still would take my hand when we crossed a busy street. This pleased me until one of them said, "Be sure to tell our mom that we remembered to help you cross the street."

This year again we are bracing ourselves for the descent of 340 pounds of human energy. We have been getting letters telling us how they've grown, along with pictures to prove it.

We know their TV viewing time is to be limited, that they may have only sugar-free gum, and that we must hold the reins on their choice of cereals. Those are some of the restrictions, and they're easy. I could figure out those for myself. What we need is a list of allowables and a few suggestions on what to do with them while they are here.

I wish I were more like my mother. She could think up more games than Goodson and Todman. But how can you tell a kid today to go slide down a cellar door or shout down a rain barrel? And can't you just see them sitting in the shade braiding clover into necklaces and bracelets?

I see the tables turning. If they can help me cross the street, they can let me take a nap. I'll sit quietly while they read to me, and when they've finished, they can pop some corn for me. After that, they can decide which TV programs I may watch.

One year I took two of them shopping. It was after their first day of the new school year, and they each had a list of the supplies they would need. We bought colored pens, spiral notebooks, and metric rulers. So much for the academic requirements.

"How about a nice pencil box?" I asked. They looked at each other before giving me the you-poor-soul look to which I've become accustomed. I was still looking at crayolas, pencils, erasers, and lunch boxes, when they moved on to another counter.

By the time I caught up with them, each had selected a round hair brush and a blow dryer. Impressed with their sales pitch on how essential these were in maintaining a neat appearance, I tossed one of each into the shopping cart. Then, seeing the ease with which this had been accomplished, my granddaughter added a brush curler, a sixty-four-ounce bottle of shampoo, and two bottles of tangle-free rinse.

I followed them around a corner, down an escalator, and through Camelot Lane, where they melted into a crowd of other children and parents. (It's not kids who get lost—it's grandmothers!) My first thoughts were that someone in the midst of this mass of people had fainted or that it was a sales demonstration. It was neither. They were all there for one purpose—to buy a pair of blue shoes with white stripes.

I thought I'd seen the same shoes stacked on a table in a drug store for $11 less, but they explained the difference to me. *These* carried a name that I can neither spell nor pronounce. When they convinced me that they couldn't walk, much less run, in any other kind, I relented.

Now out in the mall again and on a straight shot to another shop. This one was the blue denim jungle. Jeans—and nothing else. They hung from the ceiling, draped over philodendrons, and were stapled to the walls. I didn't need to be told why this was *the* place. The little four-letter word on the backside of each pair was evident.

I sat on a bench while the children went for treats. Parents and kids with sacks bigger than they were paraded past me. It was natural to think back on another time.

On my first day of a new school year, a pencil, a tablet, the new schoolroom, the new teacher were all inspirations. A shiny, new pencil box was a proud possession. Textbooks weren't furnished, so there was a rush to the bookstore to exchange last year's for those needed in this school year. I always hoped there would be no more used readers so that at least one book would seem mine and mine alone.

Being a parent of a schoolchild today is not an enviable position. Being a *grandparent*, I decided, was one of the few rewards in growing old.

All in all I have loved being a grandparent. It wasn't until I read a book on grandparenting that I had any doubts concerning my ability to fill this role. Before I'd finished the first chapter, however, I was emotionally drained. By the time I had finished the whole book, I was sobbing. I haven't cried so hard since I read *Stella Dallas*.

My reaction, I'm sure, was not the author's intent. He believes in grandparents, and it's obvious that he hopes they are here to stay, but in the meantime he would like to see them making contributions to a new type of extended family. He aims to show grandparents how they can enrich their lives, yet on almost every page there are overtones.

He would remind us that old models do not fit this new plan, that we don't know the language, and that old guidelines no longer exist. And he warns us not to fall into the trap of being oversolicitous, and finally, he says we can never make a mistake by keeping quiet. All a very discreet way of saying, butt out!

After my children were born, I supposed that some day they would grow up, have children of their own, and then I would be a grandmother. I expected to once again experience the fun of having little ones around the house, and this time it would be even better.

These grandchildren would come to visit, and when I tired of them, I would send them home. I was told that I would partake of all the joys and none of the heartaches, share in the dividends but not the responsibilities — and I fell for it.

I have given my grandchildren both quantity and quality time. Long ago I learned that unless I make it worthwhile, they will set their own limits.

I have gone from January to June trying to remember the color of their hair, but never once did I suggest they remove their radio earphones.

I've loved them from the start, and it always seemed that being a grandmother — even a *good* grandmother — was a cinch. It came naturally. Now I'm learning that love and nature aren't enough.

When I planned an Easter egg hunt, "painted" Santa Claus faces on hundreds of sugar cookies, sat on a hard boat seat eating soggy sandwiches, and trudged along a swampy riverbank in search of a baby turtle, I assumed I was a grandmother for all seasons.

This grandparenting book, like many other things in my life, was too much. And too late.

Mothers cry. So do grandmothers. For many reasons, we cry. Sometimes we cry for joy; sometimes we cry because we know no better weapon. And sometimes we cry simply because we just can't help it.

Some mothers cry when their children start kindergarten. This has always baffled me. For the oldest child and the youngest and for all those in between, there is an equal amount of weeping.

Tearful and red-eyed, they describe this somber yet unavoidable experience:

"I took him to the door, and as I walked backward away from him, he kept waving his little hand."

"He looked so tiny standing there in that big room with all those other children."

"When I kissed her goodbye, I saw her chin quiver."

"She wasn't ready for school. I felt like an ogre making her go."

"He was so eager, it was like he wanted to leave home."

"The teacher has been there so many years, she's probably callous to a homesick child."

"The teacher is so young. I wish she had more experience."

When my children started to school, I didn't picture it as such a melodrama. I didn't cast myself into the role of the villain. I kept thinking of the many times I'd searched in vain for a babysitter. I dwelled on the oatmeal I had scraped from the highchair, the crushed crayon I had picked out of the carpeting, and the seemingly endless stream of little people who wandered in and out. Mostly I remembered the "we don't have anything to do" days.

Now they had something to do. For two heavenly hours each day, they had something to do.

At some point in their child-rearing days, all mothers cry. The first haircut, the first loose tooth, the first letter from camp—all these bring a lump to a mother's throat.

I know a mother who stood at the window and watched her son set out on his paper route. When he wheeled his bike out of sight, she shed real tears. She also told me that the time she found him pinning a boutonniere to his T-shirt she got all choked up, and when he refused to change into a suit jacket, she actually sobbed.

The first time I saw my daughter's skinny legs in a pair

of nylons I cried. The cumbersome class ring (wound with miles of twine to make it fit) she wore on her left hand for a short time really broke me up.

One day I found a note on the kitchen counter. It read, "Mom, I'm playing tennis. I'll be home before dark." Somehow that little note was saved and showed up again many years later. By then an ocean separated us. I knew she would not be home before dark that night . . . or the next. I cried. Believe me, I cried.

So, we mothers cry, but not on the same occasions. Just as the things that make us happy are varied, so are the things that tug at our heartstrings.

AUNT CASSIE

Aunt Cassie is one of those more fortunate elderly ladies who have managed to go on living in their own homes. It takes a fair amount of pluck and grit to do this, and a little bluffing and stubborness can't hurt. Aunt Cassie is amply endowed with all these.

She says, "The only way 'they' will move me out of this house is feet first." Knowing she means what she says, "they" never pressure her.

She scoffs at the rubber gloves I wear for lowly household chores. She returned the electric blanket she had received as a gift and used the refund for something she needed.

As she sat doing handwork one day, she kicked aside the footstool I offered her and explained these rejections with "Once people start pampering themselves, that's when they start going downhill."

She makes clear her aversion to automatic washers when she says, "I don't need no buzzer to tell me when it's time to stop washing and time to start rinsing."

Aunt Cassie watches very little television, but has her radio running all day. She reasons like this: "When I hear somebody on the radio I really like, I don't want to be disappointed when I see them on TV."

Although she "don't cotton much to this ERA thing,"

she won't stand by and see women put down. In their defense, I once heard her say, "Let 'em think what they want, but I never did see a *woman* come out of church wearing another person's hat."

Someone said that Aunt Cassie's zest is due to her many hobbies. "What hobbies?" she asked. "I got no hobbies. I've been doing these things all my life."

She doesn't see retirement as a landmark. She can't understand why some people think this time in life should indicate a change of any kind. "I don't see why you should all at once start making candles if you never made them before."

Of loneliness she says, "Sure, I've been lonely—lots of times. But I never bothered anybody with it."

Of fear she says, "Of course I've been afraid, but when something scares you, that's the mountain you'd better climb."

Aunt Cassie says a lot of things, and when she does, people listen. And heed.

I've been listening to Aunt Cassie for a long time. Every summer, year after year, I used to spend a part of my school vacation paying Aunt Cassie a visit.

Being a guest in Aunt Cassie's home was no valid reason to do what she called "shirking your duties." She had a theory that working togther was just as much fun as playing together, and said, "If we all pitch in, we'll be done in no time."

On the first morning of my sojourn she'd say, "Now then, I've got a nice little job for you." To me a job was a job—none of them nice, none of them little. I approached each of these chores aimlessly. Every day ended in default, and every day Aunt Cassie shook her head and said, "You just don't go at things right."

There was the fresh leaf lettuce "straight from the garden" that I washed under the backyard pump—then walked away, leaving it to wilt in the sun.

Once I spilled blueing into the rinse tubs and all the white linens had to be "run through" again.

There were the pickled pigs' feet that I fried because they appeared to need something, and I didn't know what.

Related Subjects

One day I was left to watch Aunt Cassie's bread. When it was doubled in bulk, I was to put it in the oven. By the time I remembered this burden, the loaves were much too fat. I took care of it by pressing down hard on each loaf with the palm of my hand.

After they were baked, the flat-topped loaves puzzled Aunt Cassie... but not for long. When she started brushing the tops with melted butter, she saw the imprint of my hand.

"Girl," she sighed, "you just don't go at things right." Then she turned the loaf on its side, sliced off the heel, spread it with strawberry jam, and handed it to me.

Aunt Cassie was never big on the "I love you"s, but with homemade bread and jam, who needed them? She was, and is, a no-nonsense lady. To this day, she dotes on no one.

I was to remember this many years later when I called her long distance. Her phone rang several times before she answered it.

"I hope I didn't call at a bad time," I said.

"Well, you did. Another half-hour and the rates would be on."

At least she didn't tell me that I don't go at things right.

The tables have turned. About once a year, Aunt Cassie pays us a visit. Usually she comes by bus, but one year she flew because she didn't want people thinking she wasn't "up with the times." But last summer she chose the bus again, because it gives her more time to get acquainted with fellow passengers.

I was waiting at the depot when the bus pulled in. The doors opened and people started debarking. One unfamiliar face after another, but no Aunt Cassie. Then I saw the old straw suitcase on the platform, and I knew she must be somewhere. So I stepped into the bus, and there she was, gathering up her knitting bag, her hand-tooled purse, and a shopping bag full of cucumbers. As we started down the aisle, she explained, "I was teaching my new crochet pattern to that lady sitting next to me." Then, cupping her hand around one side of her mouth, she added, "She still hasn't got it, but I gave her my address so she can write if she gets stuck."

At the exit she turned to wave good-bye to those staying on the bus, and out on the platform she had to find the bus driver and thank him for a safe trip.

When finally I had her and her wares loaded into the car, I reached over to fasten her seat belt. She waved me away with, "I don't need any straps to hold me in, and I'd thank you if you'd shut off that air thing and open the windows."

Before we were out of the parking lot she said, "Stop somewhere so I can get some crochet thread and some dry mustard. I hope it won't take too long, because the Beverly Hillbillies come on in forty minutes. Tomorrow, first thing, I'll make up these cucumbers into mustard pickles. You can be doing your writin' while I do that."

"Aunt Cassie," I said, "I hate telling you this, but we just do not care for mustard pickles."

"Come next winter, you'll care for 'em. Martin can scrub the cucumbers for me. Won't take long—then we can take a drive."

The next morning I wakened to the pungent and unmistakable aroma of mustard. In the kitchen, I found Martin at the sink scrubbing cucumbers and Aunt Cassie at the stove boiling fruit jars.

It was a long two weeks. Even so, we urged her to stay longer, but she said she had a schedule to keep. A week or so later, we received this letter from her.

>Dear Ones,
>Why do you think you always have to call me as soon as I get home? Of course I got here OK. Where else would I go? It's such a waste of money.
>Like I told you on the phone, the bus was on time and my neighbor met me. I thank her for that but I don't think she took very good care of my plants.
>I had a fine time on my visit with you even if you did tell me I get on your nerves sometimes. Your Uncle Ned (God rest his soul) always said I was bossy, but I always said "Ned, somebody's got to take the reins around here." Anyway I might as

well tell you that the way you go at things makes me nervous, too.

It did make me feel good when you said I had more pep than you two put together, because it's true. And I want to thank you for my birthday party while I was there. It's good you had it this year. Some of you might not be around next year. We never know.

I didn't like seeing those coffee stains on that lace tablecloth I made for you when you got married. If you'd put it to soak right away, they'd have washed out. It's too late now.

Serve those mustard pickles the next time you have company and have a baked ham with them.

Love,
Aunt Cassie

P.S. When you write to me be careful what you say because I read all your letters to my friends.

The day we received the letter there was also a letter from Martin's Uncle John. When we'd finished reading both, I sighed, "Thank heavens they won't be coming at the same time this year."

"That happened only once," my husband replied, "and then it was just a coincidence."

"Once was enough, and it was a catastrophe."

I wasn't likely to forget those two weeks of my life. They arrived the same afternoon—first Aunt Cassie, and a couple hours later Uncle John. Aunt Cassie said, "How are you, John?" and Uncle John said, "Good to see you, Cass."

Chitchat over dinner was good natured enough. They agreed it was a fine dinner and that we "got a nice place here." Then Martin turned on the evening news and blew the whole thing.

They started with Chancellor versus Cronkite and ended with Truman versus Dewey. They took turns turning the TV volume up, down, and off. Finally Uncle John knocked the fire from his pipe, grunted, "Hr-r-r-mph," and went to bed. Aunt Cassie had won the first round.

The next morning Aunt Cassie was frying bacon when Uncle John peered over her shoulder and said, "I like my eggs basted, but not in all that grease."

"I cooked for Ned for forty-five years, and he never once complained."

"That doesn't mean he didn't want to."

Technically I suspect this round would have gone to Uncle John had Martin not appeared with the morning paper at that moment.

Every day there were issues—always something that needed settling. When Uncle John said he remembered the year 1935 when it snowed for twenty-two consecutive days, Aunt Cassie said it was more like seventeen days and the year was 1936.

She said taking a half-mile walk was beneficial, and he said it wasn't worth the shoe leather. Staunchly each morning he took his vitamins while Aunt Cassie sneered and said if he'd eat right he wouldn't need them.

One night in our own room, I said to my husband, "I'm either going into hysterics or a deep depression, I'm not sure which. I swear those two delight in sniping at each other."

"You're forgetting how old they are."

"Well, I'm not exactly Brooke Shields, you know. One of these days they're going to carry that needling too far."

"Let 'em go to it," Martin said. "They're having the time of their lives."

I learned how right he was the day our guests left for their homes. Only minutes before they would board separate planes, Uncle John couldn't resist one more bit of badgering.

"Cass," he said, "I've been wondering. How old are you by now?"

Aunt Cassie picked up her shopping bag, took a few steps toward the ramp, then turned and said, "I'll tell you that when you tell me why you never married." Then, smiling, she added, "John, you take care now."

"You too, Cass," he muttered. "You, too."

In the Gloaming, Oh, My Goodness!

Long ago I promised myself that once I was free of the eight-to-five whirligig, I'd take time to stop and smell the roses or the daisies or whatever it is we're supposed to do to wrench all we can out of these golden years.

I also made a secret vow that never, at any age, would I adopt peculiar habits.

Out of my childhood, there's a lingering memory of an elderly lady who read billboards. Often my parents took her for a Sunday afternoon ride, and she read road signs all the way. My mother might say, "It's a nice day for a drive." And this lady would answer with, "H–m–m–m–m . . . Acme Plumbing. I declare."

We had a neighbor who carried her purse over her arm wherever she went. I mean from room to room in her own home.

I also have recollections, though veiled, of a great-uncle who hummed, "Oh my darling, oh my darling, oh my darling . . ." then he'd stop – and start all over. I never did figure out what he had against Clementine.

So I've kept a close check on myself to make sure that I didn't become a victim of one of these eccentric traps.

But lately I've been worried about me. I find myself doing something I've never done before. I'm making too many observations and drawing too many conclusions.

The part that bothers me about this is that it is all so senseless. The world and I will be no better because of them. Here are a few samples:

I notice that women leaving a beauty shop hold their heads higher than they did going in.

If the driver of the car in front of me is sitting bolt upright and wearing a hat straight on his head, he'll make a left turn without signaling.

Weather forecasters who try to be funny are actually just stalling for time until they can find Delaware on the map.

"Why am I doing this?" I ask myself. "Am I getting kinky?"

One day I asked a friend what she thought. She said, "No, of course you aren't kinky. You're just a very critical person. You always have been."

So I go on, filling my spare moments with doltish thoughts, but occasionally I double my pleasure with some weightier riddles.

Sometimes I think about all the men and women whose contributions to the development of this great nation have never been chronicled.

History books are chock-full of tales of brave men. We recognize the valor of every frontiersman from Christopher Columbus to Neil Armstrong, every warrior from George Washington to Dwight Eisenhower. But how about the little guy who was the first to eat an egg?

I don't care whether it was boiled, poached, shirred, fried, or eaten raw, the first egg eater was one courageous soul. Wherever will we find a person with a stouter heart (or stomach) than this person had?

The first man who ever stepped into a barber chair and allowed a stranger to come at him with with a straight-edge was one plucky individual. Those who were the first to be hypnotized or tattooed were far from cowardly, too.

In 1920 women yielded to the latest craze and had their hair bobbed. They knew they'd be subjects of ridicule and

In the Gloaming, Oh My Goodness! 61

mockery, but one by one, then in droves, they succumbed to the tonsorial artist. Who was the first to take such a step? We'll never know, though women today are still in her debt. Sacrificing her waist-length tresses, which once held plumes and fancy combs, she walked away singing "Ain't We Got Fun." Some kind of lady.

Ten years earlier, some 15,000 women marched down New York city's Fifth Avenue to demand an American right heretofore denied them. One lady, carried away by this newly felt emancipation, wore a peekaboo blouse. Who was she? Who knows! But good for her!

With our overactive media today, these mortals would never have become forgotten heroes. Flag-waving people today are never overlooked. Tiny ripples become mountainous waves. An item scarcely newsworthy in the beginning often becomes a grave issue. The great number of married women who have either joined today's work force or are in some other way achieving their dreams are getting more than their share of ballyhoo. Their husbands are expected to approve, respect, make fewer demands, and take over at least half of the family responsibilities. Out of all that has been written on this subject, a new expression has been added to our jargon—"the supportive husband."

I keep thinking about this. I try turning it over in my mind, putting myself into the role of a young woman today, but I still don't get it.

Yesterday if a man brought home the bacon and the paycheck, he was a good husband. He was a "good provider." So I guess he, too, was a supportive husband—in his time.

So by reversing my thinking, I find that almost anything that seems offbeat today can be paralleled or even rivaled.

When I read that someone has been picked up for possession of a controlled substance, I know I cower a little. But not for long. We are, forever and always, trying to control *something*. Once we tried to restrain the use of another substance with something called prohibition. You know how that ended—"Knock twice, and ask for Gus."

Before our homes had electric outlets in the walls, we

had to plug the iron into a socket that hung from a cord in the center of the room. And to enable us to have proper light, we used a double socket—the iron plugged into one and a light bulb into the other. As we worked, the whole deal swayed back and forth with every movement of the iron. As a result bright lights and dark shadows flickered and floated across the ceiling and all about us.

I'm not sure this was the beginning of psychedelic lighting, but it's the first I can remember.

And so I ask, "What's new?" What's new is the controversy between women who work outside the home and those who don't, and I swear, once again, I don't understand this uproar at all.

On the one hand, we have the career woman who feels she must justify the hours she spends away from her home and family. On the other, there's the stay-at-home who resents being called a housewife. Their claims and disclaims are needless. Reading them is tiresome. All of them seem to be on the defensive. Why?

Whether the basis for the lifestyle each pursues is financial or personal, the path she has chosen has been her decision. She has her reasons, and they need no vindication.

What happened to being your own person, "I've Got to Be Me," and seeking one's own identity? I was just beginning to get used to everyone doing one's own thing. Now I'm wondering if it's grown a little thin. Maybe it's time to return to "sweeping your own doorstep" and "to each his own."

With all this choosing sides, you'd think the whole female population was divided into two parts—those who stay close to the nest and those who don't. A distinct misconception! There are a lot of us still hanging in there who fall into neither of these categories.

Once, we, too, were divided into two segments. Some of us worked outside the home, some of us didn't. Whichever, our reasons were unmistakable. Either we needed extra cash or we didn't. It was as simple as that. In those days, there seemed to be no other reason for anyone to "work out." It was an accepted conclusion, and no one questioned it.

In the Gloaming, Oh My Goodness! 63

Attitudes vary with the times. An awful lot depends on what needs fulfillment—we or our pocketbooks.

I'm sure this will come like a glass of ice water in the face, but it needs to be said. Whether we have chosen to be a chairman of the board or a full-time homemaker, sooner or later, regardless of the times, like it or not, there comes a day when each of us remains, or once again becomes, a *housekeeper!*

Everyone, it seems, is on the move today, and in a hurry to get there. Heaven knows I'm not the only one who dwells on this. Almost everyone agrees there is too much competition, too many activities, too much regimentation in our lives. We are being pressured with demands on our time and an appeal to give more of ourselves, yet somehow we manage to squeeze it all in without falling apart.

Granted, there are times when we are in a tizzy. There are times we are in a state of frenzy, but I see nothing that equals the hysteria of years ago when someone looked out a window and yelled, "Good gosh, we got company!"

In those days, there were two kinds of company; the expected and the unexpected. For those who were expected, the latchstring was really out. The "stage" had been set, and each member of the "cast" knew his part.

Before the unexpected guests reached the door, the reluctant hostess had ripped off her apron and swiped at a tabletop. While she straightened curtains and shoved chairs into place, she shouted instructions: "Dad put something on those bare feet. You kids pick up your toys, comb your hair and go to bed without being told, and somebody put a clean rug by the door."

All this was just for the family who lived down the road. If the visitor was the schoolteacher, she asked, "Do you kids know something I don't?"

If it was the preacher making a call, she warned, "Mind your language." If the preacher's wife had come along, she made a dash for the bedroom to pull on her corset.

I shouldn't be at all surprised if this painful reaction to outsiders was the very reason doctors stopped making house calls. They came to realize their presence within the home was just too much for all concerned.

Once this good man had been summoned, poor little Johnny was lifted, flushed and feverish, from his bed while Grandma and Aunt Maude changed the sheets. Mother came running with her best pillowcases and the white bedspread, then back to the kitchen where she poured disinfectant into the sink drain. Johnny's sister swept the porch and down the steps, while his father, who had just returned from work, changed his shirt. Then all of them stood around sad-eyed and anxious until the doctor arrived.

It wasn't that their way of life was grubby. They wanted to offer their best, their finest, but these were not a part of their daily existence.

You and I make no pretense of such perfection, do we? Now we work very hard at being *casual*.

As I let my mind wander, I find that more often than not, I am subconsciously steering my thoughts into worthwhile channels. I know I can't change the state of Union. I know there are plenty of high-salaried people in Washington trying to solve the country's problems, so why should I offer to do it for nothing? Yet, there is one problem — one very big problem — that no one does anything about. That's the zucchini squash. I wonder why no one sees the need to stamp out this prolific, spongy, overestimated green monster.

What this country needs is a recipe for something — anything — that lists zucchini as its prime ingredient. I know there are recipes for breads, cakes, cookies, and casseroles, but we're never going to get anywhere, never will we get on top of this thing, using a cup of sugar, four eggs, and one teaspoon of shredded zucchini squash.

To me, the disgusting thing about zucchini is that it asks so much and gives so little. It's so dependent. It relies on other commodities — tomatoes, onions, sugar, meat stock, bread crumbs, eggs, celery, herbs, and spices — for flavor. We peel, slice, blend, and presoak. Bake, fry, stir, and steam. We're even trying it raw, cutting it into sticks and dipping it, knowing full well that almost anything is edible with seasoned sour cream.

What we should do is sock this overindulged vegetable right in its pulpous middle and say, "Nobody likes you. You know that, don't you?"

It's the same old story of supply and demand. Have you walked through a garden lately and seen the way zucchini grows? It doesn't stand upright and honest like the other growing things. No! It lurks and skulks there, partially hidden under giant green leaves. Overnight they multiply and reproduce. They know no shame.

We got ourselves into this. We should have known. Any time someone wants to *give* us something we should be skeptical. People simply don't go around peddling stuff for free if there's any demand. And you've probably noticed that zucchini donors never ask, "Would you like one?" They say, "Here, take these."

And that's the way it is. No one can say no to a zucchini.

Since my friend assured me that I am not becoming kinky, I have allowed myself more time for this kind of meditation. I don't sit behind closed doors with the palms of my hands turned upwards. Nothing so contrived. There's no set time or place.

Whether I'm dusting furniture, riding in a car, baking cookies, or just walking down a street, my body motor is running but my mind is idling. This may account for the time I stepped off a curb in front of a van or the time I had trouble "shouting out" stains in my laundry with furniture polish. I may appear to be "out to lunch," but I prefer thinking of it as letting go.

Sometimes it is a puzzling thought that crosses my mind. Like the day I saw a car bearing Arizona license plates pulling a trailer loaded with four snowmobiles—heading southwest. Who among us could resist trying to figure that out?

One day I phoned my daughter, and she said, "I was just thinking about you—standing here peeling turnips and thinking about you." I'm still trying to figure out the connection.

I expect no answers. I'm not looking for solutions. I want no opinions. All I want, now and then, is a tiny space of time for uninterrupted musing. Private. Personal.

But isn't it surprising that people who would never think of opening another's mail or reading another's diary, think nothing at all of asking, "What's on your mind? A penny for your thoughts!"

I wouldn't let them in on it for a Susan B. Anthony dollar.

I suppose what happened to me not long ago was the result of one of my reveries. It's the sort of tale one usually hates telling on oneself, but revealing it is the best way I know to illustrate a point I want to make.

I was pushing a grocery cart through a supermarket and stopped for a moment in the bakery department. After deciding there was nothing there I needed, I moved on.

In the Gloaming, Oh My Goodness! 67

About halfway down the next aisle, I met the store manager. "You must be planning a very large picnic," he said, pointing to the cart I was pushing. Looking down, I saw *not* the cart carrying my purchases, but one from the bakery department piled high with hamburger buns. Dozens and dozens of hamburger buns—hard-to-move merchandise stacked into a cart to catch the customer's eye.

What a blooper, I thought later. No denying it, I had really goofed. I can't say it was my proudest moment. I admit I was frustrated and hoped no one had seen me as I returned the cart to the bakery department and retrieved my own.

But that's not what bothered me. The thing that bothered me was that the store manager hadn't thought it funny. Why hadn't he laughed? If I'd been twenty years old, he'd have howled. But he didn't. Instead, he touched my shoulder and said solemnly, "No harm done."

You may have noticed that grated Parmesan cheese and a well-advertised kitchen cleanser both are packaged in dark, shiny green containers. One night as I finished clearing the dishes, I sprinkled my sinks with grated cheese. I thought it was funny. Martin thought it was funny, and so did Herb and Edna. But when I told my young neighbor down the street, she put on her funereal face and said, "Oh my dear, what if you'd sprinkled your spaghetti with cleanser?"

The insinuation here is that incidents such as these are coincident with the later years. They would have us believe that this sort of thing goes hand in hand with "getting up there." I'll go along with that—part way.

Let's allow that these happenings occur more frequently as the years go by. (How fair can I be?) Then let me ask why, if it is normal behavior, does everyone go into a decline upon hearing of them?

One afternoon while standing in line at a church supper, I visited with the young man behind me. When finally we'd moved up to where he could see inside the door, he said, "I guess I'm in the wrong place. I've been waiting to vote." Henny Youngman would have given his violin for the laughs that kid got.

When you're young, you can stub your toe and fall on

your face—figuratively or physically—and it's a scream. A blunder is hilarious. A faux pas, cute.

See what I mean? At age twenty, everything is funny. At sixty, it's alarming, and that's why I've been concerned about the deep, profound thinking I've done. You know no one is going to say, "Helen handles everything with such mental agility." No one would ever suggest that I give a great deal of thought to a topic while others about me treat it as inconsequential. No! Never. You know what they'd say, "Yikes! She's getting kinky, for sure."

Yet some people think I make light of these golden years. They say that if I didn't keep bringing up all our little idiosyncrasies, fewer people would be watching for them. They insist I jest too strongly about the lives and times of our senior population.

How could I? I, too, am an eligible and qualified part of this group which, today, claims 24.9 million members. I rally around with the best of them for everything we've got coming to us. But, now and then, I step aside and observe.

For example, if Martin and I are staying mentally alert, why did we find the light bulb that was missing from our Christmas candelabra in a drawer with his socks?

Some of our friends, I notice, are shouting at each other. It starts with just three or four, but before the evening is over, we are all raising our voices. Why? We aren't all suffering a hearing loss. Not yet, we aren't.

Only last week, when I moved a lamp to a different table, I heard myself saying, "Yes . . . yes. I think I like you here." I have never talked to myself or to my plants, so why am I now talking to a lamp?

I write notes to myself. "Call Janie on Wednesday to wish her a happy anniversary." Then I answer it. "You called Janie on Wednesday. Anniversary was last month."

When weeding out a closet, I have always kept two sacks handy. I mark one *give away* and the other *throw away*. Now I must have a third one, labeled *think about it*.

Not funny? Does it make you wonder how many changes a body can handle and still maintain the image of someone whose parts are all functioning? Yeah . . . me,

In the Gloaming, Oh My Goodness! 69

too . . . sometimes. And that's our privilege. What we don't need is a patronizng look from those who haven't reached the Great Plateau.

Having reached this time in my life, I now find it rather gratifying to remember that I always have held elderly persons in high regard. I suppose it started with my parents teaching me to have respect for my elders, but in most instances it was the older folks themselves who inspired my admiration.

I recall two sisters, neither of whom ever had married, who shared their tiny and tidy home with the neighborhood children. With bare feet and legs dangling, we sat on their needlepoint chairs and drank orange nectar from china cups held in grubby hands.

There was no running in and out of that house. We walked in and, after our brief repast, we walked out. They were quiet ladies. Two old ladies living alone were expected to be quiet.

"You'd better run over and see old Mr. and Mrs. Moody," my grandfather would say on the first day of my visit with my grandparents. Each year, old Mr. and Mrs. Moody would tell me I'd grown, but to me they never changed. They sat on the same wooden chairs, under the same tree summer after summer.

Mrs. Moody, who was short and plump, wore her hair in a circle of braids on top. Mr. Moody's suspenders hung loosely over the hump in his back, and he shuffled when he walked. Even in his grey felt slippers he shuffled. I thought they were cute. Mr. and Mrs. Moody were a cute little pair.

When my mother's hair started to "turn," I comforted her with "grey hair is striking."

As my father's hairline receded, I gave him solace, too. "Bald-headed men are attractive," I said. "It's a sign of intelligence."

This was not a bit of whimsy. I truly felt these things. When youth and I walked hand in hand, I loved old people. Their tendencies to shuffle, become plump, silver-haired, and bald endeared them to me even more.

Grandmothers in particular were special. Grandmothers looked like—well, grandmothers. For one thing, they wore aprons—white and grey print aprons, edged in bias tape.

So, yes, a white-haired lady is beautiful. Plumpness is cute. Aprons are cozy. All these savory qualities favor only the elderly.

I still hold them in high regard. But I'd rather see one than be one.

We're Going to Get Away from It All If It Kills Us

So far old age hadn't proved to be a high adventure, but it wasn't a complete disaster, either. Almost from the beginning, my husband and I had agreed we would avoid rituals and routine in our lives. We never would allow the happenings of today become a repeat of yesterday's.

Too, we would watch our emotions. Our reactions to this world today would be neither giddy nor prudish. Somewhere, between absurdity and senility, we did find a way to act our age. We knew we were "getting on" but we thought we were shuffling in the right direction. Our children (and their children) seemed to see us in another light.

Each day brought a conflicting list of do's and don'ts and ideas about what was good for us. A bunch of inconsistent, self-appointed mentors they were, and they didn't know the difference between caring and patronizing.

Finally one of them said, "What you should do is pack up and go somewhere. *Get away from it all.*" The others nodded affirmatively. It was the first thing they had ever agreed on. We couldn't knock it.

Up until this time, camping had been our answer to getting away from it all. Personally, I feel that camping can get you away from more, and in less time, than any diversion I know. In a matter of twelve hours, camping can take me away from everything that makes my life comfortable. Some people think that camping means living in a tent. To me, camping is existing in any enclosure where you brush your teeth and fry bacon in the same room. This is the way I feel, and everyone who knows me is aware of it. Yet every year they insist on taking me camping again. Who are they? They are my loved ones. My family. The very ones who should care the most for my well-being.

I have pointed out to them the dangers, the risks involved when someone my age is marooned in acres of wasteland.

"Wasteland!" they jeer. "There's a town five miles from the campsite."

"Five miles is a long way to walk with a broken hip in the middle of the night alone."

"Who says you'll be alone?" my husband shouts. "I'll be there too, you know."

"That's double jeopardy," I answer.

I show them the silver hairs among the gold. For years I've told them that I'm too old for this kid stuff. For just as long, they have persisted in telling me it is good for me. Year after year, the fact that somehow I do live through it seems to prove their point.

Buying that seventeen feet of wallboard and plastic was never my idea. I wasn't in on that transaction, and had I been, I surely would never have chosen one with *Playmor* in big letters on the back.

On the day we left home, the sun shone in a cloudless sky. Traffic was light and the little camper tracked beautifully. After a couple hours on the road, I shut off the air conditioner, rolled down the windows, and suggested we drive a little faster.

"What's with you?" Martin asked.

"This is the new me," I answered. "By the way, if we get any guff about the likes of us pulling a camper tagged Playmor, let's just laugh it off. Some people may look on that as an amusing paradox, but I always say, you're only as old as you feel."

Getting Away from It All 73

It was late afternoon when we pulled on to the shores of Lake Minnegoochie. Martin hooked up the water and the electricity while I unbolted the little cupboard doors, stocked the little refrigerator, and set the little table under the little lamp.

When Martin came in, I was tossing a salad and humming "In the Land of Sky-blue Waters." His eyes followed me as I moved from the refrigerator to the stove to the table. When I lifted the casserole from the little oven, he said, "Well—say now!"

We were washing dishes in the little sink, when a neighbor stopped by to invite us to a sing-along campfire. Martin was explaining that it had been a long day and that perhaps another time would be better, when I interrupted with, "But, darling, you know how I love campfires. Of course, we'll be there."

Hurriedly I squeezed myself into the little bathroom, and changed to a pair of jeans, knotted my blouse to a midriff, donned my canvas calico print hat, and walked out the little door without missing the little step.

"I'm ready!" I shouted lightheartedly. "Where's the camera? I must get a picture of that sunset."

"Last year you said we had nineteen pictures of that sunset. You said, 'same sun over the same lake.' "

"I know, but this is another year."

"It sure is! Shall we take a couple of lawn chairs with us?"

"Certainly not. We'll sit on the beach like everyone else."

That night in our little bed I asked, "Isn't this cozy?"

"Goodnight, Mrs. Crusoe!"

"Goodnight, Robbie Baby!"

Strangely enough, up there in the north woods my favorite part of each day is the nighttime. The swashing of the lake lapping the shore and the breeze rustling through the birch trees are soothing sounds.

One night, however, the lullaby was punctuated with Martin's snoring and an owl's hooting.

You've heard, I'm sure, that people who snore go to sleep first. Take my word for it, it's true. Against the steady, wheezing static and the owl's rejoinder, the lake and the breeze didn't have a prayer. Consequently, I slept late the next morning and was just pulling myself together when Martin pulled up to the dock.

"Hi there," he shouted, as though we were meeting for the first time. "How's this for a beautiful morning? Didn't want to wake you when I got up, so I shot straight across the lake and had breakfast at Kathie's Place. Can that dame cook. She opened at 5:00 A.M. and was cooking breakfast for eighteen guys single-handed."

"Good for Kathie."

"You miss out on the best part of the day sleeping so late."

"I have to miss something. Believe me, I took in all there was to see and hear last night."

"I suppose I snored. I must have been overtired."

"That's your excuse. Now tell me what was that owl's problem?"

"Don't you know what that means? When an owl hoots like that, he's saying, 'Who-o-o-o, this is my territory.'"

"Too bad I didn't know. He's welcome to it."

"How about packing a lunch and dipping our lines for a few hours?"

Fishermen say things like dip our lines. They say they are going out to teach the worm how to swim. Or that they are taking a minnow for a ride. They never simply say they are going fishing. Maybe they don't want anyone to know what it is that they are trying to do.

Once in the boat, Martin becomes one big overweight bundle of authority. A real wiseacre.

"Lift your pole out of the water," he says as we're leaving the dock.

I have let out too much line or not enough. Sometimes he says, "Give me your rod, your bait's gone."

Later in sheer exasperation he commands, "Either fish or read, you can't do both."

So it goes; all afternoon it's lift that anchor and tote that pail.

It was thirty-six and one-half days of getting away from it all. Thirty-six and one-half days of recreation in that little

Getting Away from It All

vehicle, and Martin loved it even more than he had the day he bought it.

He had been so impressed with its compactness. He had said there was a place for everything. There was — everything except me.

I had thought that the first time he tried to park it he would concede that it wasn't all to be comradery and campfires. But he had calmly viewed the situation from all angles. He had meditated and maneuvered. When he finally succeeded, he said only that it had been a little tricky.

When the sink plugged up, the toilet ran over, and he bumped his head on a low cupboard, he blamed only himself. The barking dog next door was annoying, but its owners were mighty fine people. His only comment on the loud, wee-hour party across the lake was "live and let live."

"Wasn't it great?" he said to me at the breakfast table on our first morning home.

I looked around at my homey, familiar surroundings and answered, "Yes, it really is."

"People who don't get away like that are really missing something. But then, we don't miss what we've never had."

"On the other hand," I said, "we who do get away miss what we have had."

"I don't get it."

"Watch this," I said as I tossed eggshells into the disposal and snapped the switch.

I started the washer and dryer. I turned on the blender, the mixer, and the TV. For every outlet, there was a plug. It was a joyous choir of humming and buzzing.

I swept the floor and cried, "Look! No sand." I emptied the refrigerator trays and gloried in the amount of glistening, frozen cubes. I turned on faucets and marvelled at the water pressure. Beautiful!

"You hate it. You really hate it, don't you?"

"Actually, I don't," I said. "Getting back to nature has its points. It makes civilization look very good."

I didn't tell him that it made my life at home a palatial existence. I didn't tell him I'd given up on the idea of redecorating and building on for an office and a laundry room. Once he knows this is what thirty-six and one-half days of getting away from it all can do for me, he'll want to stay all summer. I had other ideas. As soon as I felt assured the Social Security checks would continue to arrive regularly, I started a search for *my* place in the sun.

Four hours in the air and there I was. Everything I'd been reading about was here, beckoning to me in flashing neon. Heated pools! Wooded lots! No closing costs! Nature trails! Golf, tennis, biking, fishing, and sailing!

"How about shuffleboard courts?" I asked one proprietor.

"No shuffleboard," he replied.

I said, "We'll take it." And we did.

Friends back home wrote about the mild winter they were having. Some of them had done their Christmas shopping wearing only a suit or a sweater. I wrote to them and told them I was drying my hair outside. I told them we'd tossed out our vitamin C tablets and were picking oranges through the kitchen window.

One morning a lady fresh from the beauty shop wheeled by on her bike. "Aren't the Joshua trees glorious today?" she trilled, each word on high C. As she pedaled on I watched her waving and calling to everyone she passed. "There's a woman," I thought to myself, "who could scarcely wait to grow old."

There were a lot of No Pets and No Children signs posted. Yet half the folks I chatted with said, "We dearly love animals, but . . ." Or, "Where we were last year there were so many children . . . *lovely* children, but . . ."

Our first night there, we were invited to a get-acquainted community dinner. We were greeted with, "Well, well! Here are two more who finally felt the sand in their shoes."

Someone said, "Who says a fixed income has to cramp your style? *Life*style, that is!" Then everyone laughed. Lots of cutesy little remarks like that.

But I kept telling myself it was nice. Nice to be among people of our own age. It was a coming together of white hair, bald heads, varicose veins, and pop-bottle eyeglasses—except for one couple. They looked like Donny

Getting Away from It All

and Marie with small teeth. I was relieved when I learned they were visiting their grandparents and would be leaving the next day.

So I had found a place in the sun, but at this point I wasn't at all sure it was *my* place.

One of the features promised us in this little nest in the West was friendliness. They kept their word. We couldn't have asked for more friendliness. A little less, maybe, but not more.

Supposedly this was a place where one could live the active life of leisure. *Active* is the key word. If it's leisure you want, park your car around the corner, turn off the lights, and take the phone off the hook.

I had long forgotten the irresistible urge I had to scratch my head or the center of my back when my mother stood me on a chair to pin a hem in my dress. But my first day in a ceramic class, it all came back to me.

A sewing class held in the next room was my other choice. Luckily I heard the hum of the sewing machines when I entered the building. The director must have noted my sudden pallor, because she took my arm and said, "Or would you rather sign up for ceramics?" I'd have signed up for a safari with Marlin Perkins at that point!

They had a slogan: Quit Work, But Don't Stop Living! Until then I thought I had quit work. These people were like a faulty motor—afraid to stop lest they can't get going again.

Then there were the bargains. A reduced rate if we wanted to have an intercom system installed, for instance. Our accommodations were so tiny we sometimes turned off our TV before we realized it was the neighbors' set blaring. We needed an intercom like we needed another social director.

We were invited to become honorary members of the May to September Club. Now I like honors bestowed upon me as well as the next one. But I'd rather qualify for some reason other than the fact I've lived a while—a long while.

There were special attractions in the park, like tennis tournaments and bridge tournaments where senior citizens could be participants or spectators.

There were two more classes offered. I decided not to attend either of them. One was Learn How to Be Friendly. By then, I knew all about that.

The second one was Learn How to Unwind. That one, I decided, I would save for the last day.

Even with all the regimented activities, when you're waiting for spring to come there is still time for lots of chitchat. We had covered everything from how it used to be to how it's going to be.

It was the widow from Lot 046 who got us going on the subject of horoscopes one day. She said, "I'm a Sagittarius, and last week my horoscope read *Take a chance on creativity. A new friend will stand out in the crowd.* That very day, a man in my weaving class winked at me across the table."

"So?" someone said.

"So the next day I read *Hobbies may lead to further romantic interests.* That's when I signed up for the woodworking class. Sure enough, there he was again, and this time we walked out together. Now look at this morning's paper. See what it tells me today? *Postpone a visit from a stranger. Flatterers may ask you for a loan.*"

"That's what I don't like about horoscopes," one of the "girls" said. "They just build you up for an awful letdown. One day they will tell you to *Set the spotlight on travel,* and the next, it's *Plan your entertainment at homebase.*"

"Right!" said the lady sitting next to me. "That's why I never read them. Reading *Make your health a priority* or *Financial matters could become shaky* does me no good. It's just more to fret about."

Now, I am as much a skeptic, as much inclined to build up apprehensions, as anyone possibly could be. Yet I have a method of interpreting horoscopes that eliminates all that.

I was born at midnight on the day that separates Aries from Taurus, so, you see, that gives me an edge. It works like this. If Aries says *Watch your spending* on the day I'd planned to supplement my wardrobe, I read on. Invariably, Taurus comes through for me with *Indulge yourself.*

Unfortunately, not everyone has this choice, so I couldn't expect these people to sanction this procedure. They'd probably think it was devious or something, so I thought it best not to explain. Instead I reached for the

Getting Away from It All

paper and said, "I couldn't start the day without my personal horoscope.

Quickly I scanned Taurus which read *A special bond of affection is building through a new social life.* Ah, here was Aries – and I read it aloud and with feeling: *DON'T be coerced into hobbies which hold no interest for you. YOU are tired of the social scene. WITHDRAW and recoup your energies.*

It was the next to the last day of our sojourn that I asked a neighbor, "How worthwhile is this How to Unwind Class?"

She said, "That depends on how much your *while* is worth." Well, you know how it is when you ask a silly question. Regardless, I went.

Any doubts I had had about how much I needed this course soon were dismissed. By the time I'd maneuvered my car through six lanes of traffic to get there, I thought I was ready for it. When I saw two women wearing cervical collars, I knew I was.

Except for those two, everyone was playing follow the leader. With arms hanging loosely at their sides, their heads rolled around and around to the clipped rhythm of "Front! Right! Back! Left!" Thinking it looked harmless enough, I joined them and was just getting the beat, when Our Leader shouted, "Oh, gotcha! That time I said, 'Front! *Left!* Back! *Then* right!'" Tricky. How could we hear her with all those neck bones crunching?

That was the opener. The next segment was devoted to sharing with each other all those little things that tied us up in knots.

"Listening to the news these days makes me very nervous," one lady said.

"Losing control, like spending so much for food, seeing our budget go down the drain," another offered.

Some thought their anxieties stemmed from their inability to accomplish as much as they once had. Several confessed an unwillingness to conform to today's standards. Facing up to physical changes was the lament of many.

Some felt the strain of too many demands on their time, whereas others had too much time on their hands.

It really was a good meeting. It had been like looking

into a mirror or hearing one's own voice. I was sorry I had contributed so little, but I was relaxed.

Our Leader then made comments and suggestions. She thanked each of us for our cooperation. She agreed that all these things are definitely and understandably tension builders; that it was natural that we, as bright and intelligent ladies, should react as we had.

She had us in the palm of her hand. At that moment there wasn't a woman in that room who would not have signed up for a twelve-month course. Then she blew it. In one sentence, she blew the whole thing.

"These," she said, "are fine examples of the pressures endured by those of you who are *rounding out your life cycle.*"

When we started on this trip, we were determined to put our worries behind us. We tried not to pack our troubles. In this home away from home, with no need to fight the elements, it should be easy to relax.

The first few days we managed quite well. But soon we were wondering if that kid remembered to stop delivering the newspapers. Would the mail be forwarded—and, if it was, would the junk be sorted out? We knew we had unplugged the coffee pot and turned back the thermostat, but did we close the draperies? I, of course, carried it one step further with "What if the pilot light on the furnace should go out?"

Next door was a gentleman who had the pluck to make the move permanent. "One winter out here and I knew this was it," he said, netting one leaf at a time from his swimming pool. "I wish I'd known then what I know now. I'd never buy another place with deciduous trees. Leaves in a swimming pool are a darn nuisance."

The current status symbol that winter was the solar energy system. Without a King Kong erector set on your roof, what is there to talk about? Once it's up there, however, the days without sunshine are dark and gloomy.

Besides the novices like us and the stronghearted who had settled in, there was another little group—the preretirees. These were the people who are not yet old enough to retire. We knew this because they kept telling us so. They were out there just trying it on for size, they said.

Getting Away from It All

I wanted to tell them that they couldn't know how it would be until they really got there. I wanted to tell them not to believe everything they read. I wanted to warn them that the move into retirement is not a smooth transition. And I wanted to do it in a way that wouldn't make me a skeptic in their eyes.

I hadn't always been such a hard nut to crack. Once I was an easy mark. I believed in the tooth fairy, the Easter rabbit, Santa Claus, and Dorothy's looking glass. Doggedly, I washed my face with soaps that were sure to give me that schoolgirl complexion or the skin you love to touch, and I didn't care which came first. Later I saw the USA in my Chevrolet, and I never kept bananas in the refrigerator.

I pledged allegiance to my flag, my country, to Harry Truman (and Margaret), the NRA, the PTA, and to every huckster who ever ballyhooed a product.

Then came the time when I needed new direction. People were asking what I would do after I retired, and I hadn't an answer. As Will Rogers said of newspapers, all I knew was what I read in magazines.

They told of families who ran together. Three generations in baggy, cotton-knit suits panting down the road together.

With the aid of group-buying power, retirees were traveling. There were short cruises and long cruises. From eastern ports and western ports.

I poured over pictures of couples skimming across dance floors and jetting across continents or just walking hand in hand through prairie grass. And yet another couple—and this pair I will never forget—sacked out under a palm tree, wearing cardigans with the creases still in the sleeves and the first pair of sneakers they'd ever owned.

All of it dreamy, intoxicating, *misleading*.

Wherever we journey, we'll wonder if we closed the draperies back home. Misgivings travel with us. A change of geography won't stop the passing of the years.

We may get away from a lot of things, but we can't get away from it all.

Not Like the Ones We Used to Know

At the beginning of each Christmas season, there is an atmosphere of benevolence and generosity. Before it's over, there is something else in the air, and it isn't a song.

We start by opening our hearts and our pocketbooks. Fervently we conspire, project, and prepare. We reach for the unattainable.

We ask more of ourselves than we are able to give. When we see time is running out and we are far from our goal, we become snappish. We complain and grumble, "It's all just too commercial."

True, every year the fact that the holidays are coming is proclaimed a little earlier. Merchants have their wares shoved, jammed, and wedged into every available space, and they're using every gimmick known to lure and entice us.

Almost before we've finished raking the leaves, store windows are filled with sparkling and tantalizing gift-boxed items. Their catalogs are out, their doors open twelve hours a day sometimes, seven days a week, and we sigh, "It isn't like it used to be."

Not Like the Ones We Used to Know 83

We sit back and picture a time when it took so little to make us happy. We can see it yet as if it were yesterday—sleigh tracks in the snow, wild geese in flight, children skating on a frozen pond, a church steeple against a winter sky—all that heartwarming stuff that greeting cards are made of.

Less happily revived are the memories of drafty rooms, poorly stocked shops, food shortages, and the long wait between paydays.

In comparison I feel rather pampered as I browse through the stores today. I am both amused and enthralled with the extravagant decorations, animated, splendid, and gaudy.

I like walking on carpeted floors, people-watching in the malls. I appreciate the nearby coffee shops, the too handy credit cards, and the carols by Muzak.

So, what of all the commercialism? Are we so caught up in tinsel materialism that we are forgetting what we are really celebrating? Is it taking the place of the true meaning of Christmas? Not unless we allow it to.

We can shop early, at the last minute, or not at all. The season is getting longer every year. The time is ours to apportion as we wish.

We're free to shout Happy Hanukkah, Merry Christmas, or Bah, humbug!

There's nothing to say that we must conform. We aren't forced to fall in with the conventional—and thank heavens for that!

If there's anything worse than standing by and watching your grown children make their own mistakes, it's watching them build their own traditions, particularly at Christmastime.

I'm not mulish and dead set in all the old ways. I see the wisdom in the man-made, flameproof Christmas tree, even though I wistfully envision a pine chopped down in the woods and dragged home through the snow in mittened hands.

I need to watch the calories as well as anyone, but when I bite into a papaya-sunflower seed cookie, the yearning I feel for one of Grandma's old-fashioned soft sugar cookies is next to unbearable.

We used to take snapshots of the family around the tree. The small children were a sugarplum vision in pinafores, ruffles, creased slacks, and shiny shoes. I gave up on this when I had trouble blending jeans, crew neck sweaters and boat shoes with a holly and glitter background.

Today parents don't sit down together and talk over what they will give their offspring for Christmas. There's nothing to talk about. Long before Christmas the kids have taken the guesswork out of it. Conversely, in some families the children aren't included in pre-Christmas plans. No construction paper cutouts pasted to the window panes in this home. The decorations are an affluent display contrived for adult show and tell. I know a mother who each year chooses one new and very special ornament for *her* tree. It hangs there among the others like a precious jewel. Elegant. Not meant to be touched, only admired. If it is symbolic of anything, it must be artistry.

I don't know about such things. What I understand is a string of cranberries and popcorn. No boutique item has more charm than a garland of paper circles linked into a chain.

What would it take to get the whole family around the piano to sing carols? A power failure. Nothing short of a power failure could drag them from the dark room where they are mesmerized by video games.

A tradition is an inherited way of thinking or acting. It is the handing down of beliefs and customs. The life expectancy of a tradition is very short—and getting shorter.

With all the faultfinding groups who think it is their task to make this a better, safer world, I wonder that the legend of St. Nicholas has gone unchallenged. Each year I expect someone to take exception to the notion that Santa and his miniature sleigh sail across the sky with no flight pattern and no landing clearance. As Santa whistles, shouts, and cracks a long, black whip, eight tiny reindeer take to the sky. It's all right there in words and pictures for every child to drink in. Yet there's not so much as a tsk-tsk from those concerned about cruelty to animals.

Not Like the Ones We Used to Know 85

There's prancing and pawing of hoofs on roof tops, which certainly shows disregard for another's property. The goodies left in Christmas stockings are a contradiction to never accept candy from a stranger, but so far at least parents aren't protesting.

Neither has anyone questioned the legality of all those elves who are employed in Santa's workshop. Are they organized? Are they paid overtime? Is the work seasonal and are they eligible for unemployment?

No one questions the eternal agility of this jolly old elf. Year after year he slides down the chimney to a safe landing. He tracks ashes and soot across your wall-to-wall, and he is obviously overweight. What's more, he holds the stump of a pipe tight in his teeth, and the smoke that encircles his head is enough to trigger your smoke alarm.

The well-known poem also says that the stockings were hung by the chimney, and that's the way we did it way back when. I can still see them—long, black, skinny, cotton stockings *nailed* to the back of a kitchen chair alongside the potbellied stove.

On Christmas morning, even before Papa got the stove going, we ran with bare feet across the cold floor to the living room, never doubting that St. Nicholas had been there. After a quick check to see if the stockings were bulging, we'd go on to better things.

But later in the day, after parts of games were missing, and after sleds had had a trial run, we returned to the stockings.

There would be an apple, an orange, filberts and Brazil nuts in the shell, and the candy that the grocer had given Papa the day before as a treat for paying the bill. Hard candy it was, in all sorts of shapes and colors. By now it was stuck to the stocking itself. So we'd pull it loose and lick off the black fuzz before eating it.

Through the years, few Christmas traditions have undergone the changes quite like those of the Christmas stocking. For some reason, a child's own stocking would no longer serve the purpose. The first store-bought stocking was of a coarse red mesh, not unlike that used for sacking potatoes today. There also were stockings made of red plastic with a band of real cotton at the top. Then along came the hand-knit and hand-crocheted ones. No commercialism here. There was love in every stitch as those needle-handy ladies turned out lovely, adorable creations. So the Christmas stocking has become a thing of beauty and elegance. It is embroidered, needlepointed, appliqued, and bejeweled. It hangs from the mantle by a gold ring and tassel. But heavy, heavy hangs over the child who touches it—even though his name is written on it in sequins.

I'm filled with a longing when I look back on those days when all our Christmas packages looked alike; plain white tissue paper with stickers picturing Santa Claus and candy canes concealed the gift. Paste of flour and water held it all together. The joy we felt when those artless little packages began to appear under the tree can't be duplicated, because we knew that within each homely, ill-shaped little bundle was a present: a crocheted lace collar and cuff set; a beanbag; a smooth, varnished board with a hole in it to throw the beanbag through; a powder puff enhanced with a ruffle of soiled lace, tacked on with huge stitches of red thread; the outline of a sibling's chubby hand on a sheet of yellow lined paper; a bracelet made of assorted buttons strung on a strip of narrow elastic.

How exciting it was! How thrilling to see the secret you'd been keeping for weeks finally revealed! It was one surprise after another—frenzied, magical pleasure.

More than anything I can think of, I would like a return of that kind of Christmas enthusiasm one year. I know it can't be, but if it could, that's what I would love—a return of the joyful enthusiasm of a Christmas wrapped in white tissue paper and sealed with flour and water paste.

So, yes, I must admit to a certain amount of diminishing spirit each year, and I have wondered if other persons in their mellow years share my sentiments. In a busy shopping center one day, I got my answer. They do!

The place was filled with "nice little old ladies" and "cute little old men," so eavesdropping was at its best. Their words were laced with a song in the air.

(*Do you hear what I hear?*)

Not Like the Ones We Used to Know

"Wow! That parking lot is a zoo! I drove around that thing four times before I found a space."
(*The horse was lean and lank. Misfortune was its lot.*)

"How do you know what kids want these days? All that electronic junk. I think we'll just send a check."
(*Every mother's child is gonna' spy, to see if reindeer really know how to fly.*)

"Sh-h-h! Here's the children's choir. That's our grandson — second row, fourth from the left."
(*Sing, choir of angels, sing in exultation.*)

"We've been here since morning, and she hasn't bought a thing."
(*God rest ye merry, gentlemen. Let nothing you dismay.*)

"Did you see that? That woman pushed me right out of the line. She actually shoved me."
(*Peace on earth, and mercy mild; God and sinners reconciled.*)

"We're not having a tree this year. It seems so silly just for the two of us."
(*Oh tannenbaum! Oh tannenbaum!*)

"When I took some packages to the car, I saw it had started to snow. Guess we'd better get going."
(*Snowflakes that stay on our brows and our lashes.*)

"I can't take the crowds like I used to. Once Christmas Eve gets here, I'm okay. Then things sort of quiet down."
(*The world in solemn stillness lies.*)

To each of these people, I should have said, "Thanks, I needed that." They helped me to know what I had already suspected — that I had slipped a bit in the wrong direction. At the same time, I was made to realize that, although it wasn't desirable, it was at least normal.

So glad tidings to them and to all those who are a part of today's senior population. For all your Christmases to come, I wish you joy—many joys. Joy that comes from warmth and affection. A quiet joy, both glorious and reverent.

I wish you memories—a golden collection of Christmas moments. I wish you the need to relate your recollections, and I wish you someone to listen.

Whether the view from your window is sunny and mild or blanketed in snow, I wish you comfort. I wish you good food, proper clothing, and all of your favorite things.

I wish you someone to remind you of your strength and not your weaknesses, so that you may find gladness in each season's festivities.

I wish you graciousness to receive, as well as to give, especially gifts of love.

I wish you time—plenty of time—to adjust to changes, to make decisions, and to ease your sorrows.

I wish you dreams not just of yesterday, but also of tomorrow, and the certainty and perseverance to make them come true.

I wish you more happiness and less loneliness, more fellowship and less competition.

When you are tired, I wish you contentment and peace. Peace in your home and in your heart. And I wish for peace in a world that sometimes seems a little weary, too.

I wish you Christmas trees that glisten, sleigh bells that jingle, and church bells that ring through the midnight air.

I wish that all of your days, as well as the days of Christmas, be merry and bright.

I wish you not be dispirited when you recall the simplicity of Christmas as you and I once celebrated it. If it seems that Christmas is not like the ones we used to know, I wish you abiding tolerance, for the real meaning of Christmas never changes, never ends.

Friends and Folks

JANIE

Each and every weekday, we can snap on our television sets and see nice people moving in and out of unthinkable situations. There are a few scoundrels among them, but their appearances tend to make the nice people seem even nicer. They live in nice houses, wear nice clothes, and they say such nice things.

My friend Janie could slip into one of these roles with nary a rehearsal. She looks the part. She speaks their language.

Janie loves surprising me. Following one tiny tap on my door, she opens it and sings, "Guess who! May I come in?"

While she waits for me to take her coat, I snatch curlers from my hair and clear last week's newspapers from a chair. Watching my every move, she says, "I should have called first, but I was in the neighborhood."

"That's okay. You just caught me at a bad time. Yesterday at this time, I had everything done — my housework, my hair, my makeup."

"Oh, Helen," she says, "you and I have known each

other too long to pretend. You are *you*, and I am *me*." This was Janie's soap opera way of saying, "You are a slob; I am not."

Yet I knew she was right. Had I dropped in on her unexpectedly, she would have taken my coat, and while she was putting it on a velvet hanger, she would have asked, "May I get you something?"

Seldom do I make an honest-to-goodness statement when I'm visiting with Janie. But in the few times that I have, she replied, "You can't mean that!" The next time this happens, I'm coming back with "I was never more serious in my life!" (She's not the only one who watches daytime drama.)

If I glued myself to the television set for five days in a row, I would never see anyone make a more polished entrance or exit than does Janie.

Likely you've noticed how all those soap opera Sophies wear earrings and neck scarfs at the breakfast table. I'm not sure Janie goes that far, but I do know her little feathered scuffs have never set foot on her kitchen floor.

Yet Janie is nice. She lives in a nice house, wears nice clothes, and says nice things.

One day Janie invited me to have lunch with her at her nice house. For once, I was determined to be organized so I wouldn't be rushed for time.

I did my hair and nails the night before. I steam pressed slacks that I usually pull on straight from the dryer. I wore a new sweater, which I thought I might shed during the afternoon, then fold so the label would show.

I left early enough to have time to drive through the car wash. It was just a bit foggy, so I turned on my lights. I really had it all together—as serene as Janie, herself.

She met me at the door with, "You left your car lights on." So, back to the car, where I skinned a knuckle on something and, of course, it bled—and bled. I was fumbling in my purse for a tissue, but you might know, Janie had a box of lavender ones right there handy. "Here," she said, handing me one, "take this while I run out and get your gloves. You dropped them in the driveway."

Before I had pulled off my second boot, she said,

Friends and Folks

"Guess you didn't bring any shoes, did you? Here, slip into these." I looked at the silver mesh slippers she'd brought me. Two sizes too small. Janie's husband Doug had left his size twelve, brown corduroy loafers by the door so I scuffed around in those.

In the den, Janie's black poodle, wearing a red and black plaid collar, was curled up in a red and black plaid chair. I swear that dog went with her mistress when she took those courses in interior decorating.

She served our lunch at a little round table in the niche formed by the bay windows. Sitting there, I had the feeling that at any minute, a little lady wearing a long, maroon velvet coat with matching bonnet and muff might appear.

I told Janie she had gone to too much trouble for just the two of us, but she said that actually she had slept in that morning, and Doug had made the salad. Then I said that Martin often wipes dishes for me and sometimes runs the vacuum. She said that she had a dishwasher and that the lady who cleans for her did the vacuuming.

I told her that our granddaughter had been promoted to an advanced piano class, and she said her grandchildren were both in private schools this year.

It was time to leave before I remembered to take off my sweater and display the label.

I sat down in a little chair in the foyer where I kicked off Doug's size twelves and was about to pull on my boots when I noticed a stack of addressed and stamped envelopes on a nearby table.

"Don't tell me," I groaned. "Those aren't Christmas cards!"

"Yes, they are," she purred. "Our Christmas cards are all ready for mailing.

"Sure," I chided. "All ready except for those you have to send out in a hurry when you receive one from someone you forgot."

"But I *didn't* forget anyone.

"You're sure?"

"Of course I'm sure."

"We haven't had Thanksgiving Day yet," I reminded her. "I suppose you have everything set for that, too?"

"We eat out on Thanskgiving Day."

"I tried that once. Late in the day there was a parade to and from the kitchen. They grew restless. They slumped in their chairs. They looked at me with big, sad eyes. Finally one of the grandchildren said, 'I'm hungry.' And there I was with not so much as a cranberry to offer them."

Janie laughed. "I know – my family reacted the same way the first time we went out for Thanksgiving dinner. I just looked straight at each of them and said, 'You are *not* hungry. You couldn't possibly be hungry.' That settled it."

I was stunned, but I shouldn't have been. I remember the time Janie's son said he had a stomachache, and she said, "No, your stomach is all right. You are just excited." Sure enough his stomach stopped hurting.

Janie has talked her child out of a carnival ride, sleeping in a tent, and going out for football by asking him, "You wouldn't want to make me sad, would you?"

My children always beat me to the punch with, "You wouldn't want to spoil our fun, would you?"

Sometime I may try Janie's strategy; we will all go out for Thanskgiving dinner. Mentally, I picture it. Later in the day, they will be slumping in their chairs and looking at me with beagle eyes and someone will say, "I'm hungry." I will stare at them, all of them, and say, "You are *not* hungry. You couldn't possibly be hungry."

They will start to laugh. Then when they see that I am serious, they will appoint a guardian for me.

Janie started early. She never shouted, never threatened, and there was never any actual regimentation. Always it was just warm and fervent persuasion. Concisely but quietly, Janie settles all disharmony. Then she walks away – and never looks back.

It was a momentary feeling of low spirits that prompted my spur-of-the-moment decision to stop by Janie's one afternoon. When she opened the door, I didn't greet her with a chorus of "Auld Lang Syne," even though I had something like that in mind.

I felt a need to see Janie even though I know her mild opulence is not something that leads you down memory lane. Nor is the tasteful luxury of her home a backdrop for

Friends and Folks

hashing over the good old days of one's youth. What was there, and has always been there, was the gladness of being together.

How did we happen to become friends? Was it by choice or circumstance? I mean, had we been tossed together on the sidewalks of New York instead of a protected midwestern neighborhood, would such an attachment have developed? Had we been the children of famous parents, growing up with ever-widening horizons, would our friendship have been so lasting?

We have always had our differences—differences that have been split so many times, it seems there could not be much left. So I wonder—what is the glue that has held this friendship together for such a very long time?

Probably in the early years, it took no more than a game of hopscotch or a birthday party to make us best friends. Later a mutual adoration of Tillie the Toiler, Norma Talmadge, and the new, young minister were the secrets we shared.

There were the years of rivalry when we competed for the lead in class plays and the highest score in music appreciation. We vied for being first in everything from shedding our long, heavy underwear in the spring to owning a "gold" Eversharp pen and pencil set.

When one of us married, there was, for a time, a strained interlude, but once we both became young matrons, the friendly relationship picked up almost where it had left off. We entertained bridge club, grew victory gardens, spooned up Pablum, and hooked rugs. We swapped recipes and baby-sitting.

We have endured changes, both sudden and gradual. Singularly and together, we have survived life's ups and downs. Between us there has been an ongoing exchange of consolation, sympathy, and congratulations.

During our early life, we had our childish spats. During our midlife we called them arguments. Today in later life, we still have them, but we now term them lively discussions.

I left Janie that day with a renewed awareness of what our friendship has meant to me. I wanted to say, "Janie, dear friend, I am thankful that we still have each other." But I didn't. Janie doesn't like that sort of thing. It's one of our differences.

But, like I said, Janie is nice.

EDNA

One morning my neighbor Edna came over, and we sat in my kitchen drinking coffee for an hour or more. While I folded paper napkins into tiny triangles, she shelled four quarts of peas and snapped a mountain of string beans. When she'd finished, she took another sip of coffee and said, "I must go. I've got the timer set for my beet pickles, and my bread will be ready for the oven."

After she'd gone, I sat for a time recalling that day so long ago when Edna and her family moved into the house next door.

It was on a wicked day in March that I watched the huge moving van inch its way out of traffic, back over the curb, and handily angle itself right to the door. Knowing her as I do today, I shouldn't be surprised if it were Edna herself at the wheel.

On that day, however, I felt nothing but pity for her. I pictured the frigid house, the searching for dishes, bedding, and light bulbs; the frantic mother, the disheveled father, and the cranky kids—all of them cold and hungry. I knew I must do something to help.

By late afternoon, I had put together a double recipe of chicken divan and spelled Welcome with strips of pimento across the top. While it baked, I took the curlers from my hair, did my face, and tied a pink organdy apron over my starched housedress.

I set my children up to the table and gave them cornflakes with sliced bananas and told my husband to make himself a fried egg sandwich. Then, after covering the casserole with a linen cloth, I lifted it with ruffle-edged pot holders and set out on my act of mercy.

I hoped I was not going overboard in my proficiency. I didn't want this poor woman to feel inhibited. She might

Friends and Folks

burst into humble tears, her husband might shake my hand with both of his, and the children might kiss the hem of my skirt.

What I really saw when I walked into that home for the first time was a mother, a father, and two small children, all clad in cozy, hand-knit sweaters, sitting around a dinner table laden with a home-cooked, well-balanced meal. Not a packing box was in sight. Everything was orderly and cheery. Lunch boxes were lined up against neatly stacked schoolbooks in readiness for the next morning. My chicken divan was placed in the freezer alongside labeled packages of homegrown fruit and vegetables.

This was my introduction to Edna – Super Neighbor. Since that day, I have watched her wax lawn furniture, sterilize garden tools; and steam press washcloths.

Edna is a weaver. She puts out more yardage in any given year than Fruit of the Loom.

Edna sews. She makes everything from swimsuits to fake fur coats.

Now I, myself, have a thimble with my name engraved on it. I also own scissors with gold-plated handles. And I have a wicker, velvet-lined sewing basket. All these were gifts from my optimistic mother. When I tell you that the sewing basket today contains a package of picture hooks, a green plastic bracelet, a couple of road maps, an argyle sock, and a three-cent postage stamp, you'll know that the three years I spent in home economics classes were wasted.

But I do not begrudge Edna her undeniable talent. She is my friend as well as my neighbor, so I'm always right there with a word of praise. I'll say, "Edna, I love your blouse. I'm sure it is another of your lovely creations."

Having done my part, I want her to simply say thank you and disappear.

But, no! This is her clue to reply, "Oh, yes. I got the material at a remnant sale – cost me $3.88, including the thread."

Not long ago, we spent an evening with Edna and her husband, Herb. I was sure she'd made the dress she was wearing, so I told her it was a real prize and waited for her to answer, "Cost me $1.02, including the pattern."

Instead she said, "I made Herb's suit, too. Cost $28, including the zipper."

Now you aren't going to believe this, but try—*please!* last week, Edna painted her furnace. *White!*

Edna is nice, too. Just ask anyone, and they'll tell you that Edna is a nice lady. But having her for a neighbor has never been easy.

HETTY

She was tall and angular, and her figure seemed to be more of a structure than a body. Her skin was spongy; her hair the color of dark ashes.

Her dress was made from dingy twill and would have touched the ground had it not been for the length of baling twine worn around her waist. She lived in a one-room shanty with no plumbing and no electricity at the edge of town. Her name was Hetty.

People said she had a lot of money stashed away. Some said she was a squatter, but no one ever knew for sure.

Hetty's only visitors were schoolchildren who were in need of a tutor, and Hetty was the best. In phonics and Shakespeare, times tables and geometry, she coached them patiently and tirelessly, stopping only long enough to shoo a chicken from the table where they worked.

She could name all the presidents, all the state capitals, and she knew the Gettysburg Address by heart.

They used to call her a genius. Some said she was highly educated. Others said she was self-taught, but no one ever knew for sure.

She carried a cane, but never used it. Besides the chickens, she had a few ducks, a goat, and two pigs, and the hearsay was that she talked to the animals.

Some said she was strange, even a little touched. Others thought she was dumb like a fox, but no one ever knew for sure.

Townspeople did a lot of speculating about Hetty. In the barber shop, on the bench outside the variety and dry goods store, on front porches and in backyards, they in-

Friends and Folks

vented tales. Unfounded and founded. Likely and unlikely. Once Hetty had loved and that love was not returned. She had lost a child in a tragic accident. She was the victim of amnesia. She was a Hollywood starlet seeking anonymity. She was wanted and was hiding out. There was a lot of guessing, but no one knew for sure.

One day Hetty put her old flat, black pocketbook over her arm and walked to the hospital. A few days later she died. They said the cause of death was pneumonia. Some said it was malnutrition, whereas others said her heart just plain wore out. No one knew for sure.

Word of Hetty's death filtered through the town. People wondered if she'd been ailing for long. Had she suffered? Had she left any final instructions? Was there a distant relative to be contacted? No one knew.

Had anyone befriended her these past few days—or ever? Did anyone send flowers or even a card? Would Hetty have welcomed friendship? Would she have accepted help?

No one had ever offered, so no one ever knew—not for sure.

MR. SLOAN

Mr. Sloan was my friend, and I'll never have a better one. If he had a first name, I never heard it. He was just Mr. Sloan, janitor at the grade school I attended.

Every morning and noon when the first bell rang, students from all grades lined up outside the building, waiting for the strains of "Columbia the Gem of the Ocean" to be scratched out on the Victrola with its morning-glory horn. Then Miss Conroy, who always stood at the head of the line, would snap her head toward the open door and start marking time in place.

All this was very important to Miss Conroy. To her, the perfect day was that day on which each child put his right foot forward on the first note and proceeded with toes and eyes straight ahead.

One day I turned to whisper to the girl behind me and was promptly jerked by the coat sleeve back into position.

Everyone was looking at me, and I was near tears. Then I looked up and there was Mr. Sloan. He gave me a brief smile and a quick wink. That's all it took. I knew he didn't like Miss Conroy any better than I did. At that moment, and for the next four years, he was my pal.

On my way home from school one afternoon, I discovered two pieces of chalk in my pinafore pocket. Terrified that someone would think I had stolen it, I ran back to school, reaching there just as Mr. Sloan was turning the key in the door. He took the chalk from me, assuring me that he would have it in its rightful place early the next morning.

Mr. Sloan would never ring the last bell if there was one kid in sight. I can remember how I would be racing through the school yard, while Mr. Sloan stood there, both

Friends and Folks

hands on the heavy rope. He seemed to know just how long it would take for me to hang my wraps in the cloakroom and get at least one step into the classroom. Then I'd hear the two tolls, and under my breath I'd say, "Thank you, Mr. Sloan. We licked 'em again." As I took my seat, Miss Conroy would stare at me, then glance at the clock and shake her head. Miss Conroy wasn't dumb. She was silly, but she wasn't dumb.

Besides handling his janitorial duties, Mr. Sloan was the keeper of lost mittens and marbles. Of skate keys and secrets. He knew what to do for hurt feelings, as well as for a hurt knee. He'd hold your lunch pail when it was your turn up to bat.

I guess they aren't called janitors any more. They are Superintendents of Grounds and Buildings. But in my book, a janitor by any other name could be no better guy than our Mr. Sloan.

Over What *Hill?*

During an interview a young starlet said it will give her confidence to know that she will have a following no matter how old and pitiful she becomes. Old and pitiful. Must they go together?

I know people who are old but surely not pitiful. I also know a few who are pitiful, yet — well, never mind. In the face of today's sexual permissiveness, we've let go of the concept that love and marriage must go hand in hand. Now let's do the same for old and pitiful.

We who have grown old do not need it stamped on our foreheads. We are old, and it's obvious.

"She's getting up there," someone says. Sure she is. Some of us already have gotten there.

"He's not as young as he used to be," says another. Who is?

Johnny Carson leans heavily on Burbank's prune-eating Geritol set in his monologues. "Never say 'dye' to an old person," he says, and everyone goes into hysterics.

We're a bunch of "silver domes" entering the "final stretch." We've "been to the well a coupla times." We weren't born "yesterday," and neither are we "kids" anymore.

It's no wonder that contemplating old age poses a problem. All these make it hard to find the so-called rewards in the aging process.

Can't we take a joke? Sure we can. All twenty-four million of us are rolling on the floor, but just once in a while, we'd like to be at the other end of the arrow.

A baby gurgles and spits up. The small child has a temper tantrum—screams and holds his breath. The adolescent rebels and locks himself in his room. The middle-aged woman has hot flashes while her male counterpart gets the seven-year itch. But it's no big deal. It all goes with the territory.

We oldies sometimes totter. Instead of turning our head sharply, we slowly turn our whole body. We watch our feet when we go down a flight of steps. What happens? Everyone shouts, "Hey look! He's *really* slipping."

If we're cautious, we are slipping. If we take a nap, it's not because we are sleepy—we're failing.

Know what we really, truly would like? We would love to be just one of the gang.

One day in a coffee shop, my husband and I were greeted by a young waitress with, "Hi! How are you *guys* today?" Bless her little heart, wherever she is.

Next to creaking joints, sagging flesh, diminishing vigor, and thinning hair, the thing most despised by many of us is being called a Senior Citizen.

Adjusting to these physical changes, along with a new lifestyle, we feel, is quite enough. Having to fight for our identity is heaping it on.

Although I hear opposing viewpoints on how the elderly feel about this, those who do find it distasteful express themselves rather heatedly.

"Don't you ever refer to *me* that way, or you'll answer for it," someone said to me one day.

"Trust me. I won't," I answered, backing away.

Another, less hostile but nonetheless firm, said, "It's like tossing us all into one big sack and tying a tag on it."

Others thought it suggested second rate or, at best, definitely not A-one or top of the line.

One lady, more soft-spoken than the others, commented, "I think it's better than anything starting with old—like old-timer, old codger, or old duffer."

I was talking about this with a gentleman whose opinion I have valued for a long time. He is wise, polished, seasoned, and just a little slippery.

He listened and then thought for a long moment.

"How do I feel about being called a Senior Citizen?" he asked. "Well, truthfully, I've not had the time to dwell on such things, you know. But I'd say it's not bad. Rather good, in fact. It's concise and it's collective and far less revealing than classifying us as sexagenarians, septuagenarians, or octogenarians, wouldn't you say?"

As I recall, I didn't say anything. But confidentially, I was thinking that most anything was better than learning to spell those three words.

I wonder sometimes why we have to be labeled at all. It gets to be a real drag, this being set apart from the rest of the population. I feel real empathy for young people who are tagged teenagers for seven or more years. Sooner or later though, they will grow out of it, whereas we grow only deeper into it.

In many ways, we are a funny lot. We know we're aging, but we can't quite face up to aged. We'd rather be in the process than the finished product.

We love to brag about our grandchildren, but we don't want to *look* like a grandparent. We are a little smug when we say, "I'm not your average grandparent. I don't do babysitting." Then we are jealous when grandchildren become attached to a sitter our own age.

When there's a need for soliciting, canvassing, campaigning, or getting involved in any of those thankless jobs, we say, "I've gone that route. Call someone younger." When they do, we sit back and feel neglected.

We defend ourselves with, "Listen, I'm not as young as I used to be. I need my rest." Then, along with our peers, we take off for Vegas for four days and three nights of debauchery, plus night flights coming and going.

Seems like no one ever tells us that we are pretty or handsome these days. But when, occasionally, someone does come up with a bit of flattery, we doubt their sincerity.

Over What Hill?

We think they're trying to boost our morale.

We shout, "Just wait 'til you're seventy years old!" In the next breath, which we're not sure will ever come, we whisper hoarsely, "and if you tell anyone I'm seventy years old, I'll strangle you." We blow hot and cold.

Because we've lived these many years, we think we are entitled to certain rights. We want our rights. Rights, but not wrinkles.

One of the rights we think is due us is the right to be a little less than honest at certain times.

No one, man or woman, could have endured the rigors of the past sixty years and remained the virtuous and upright citizen he or she started out to be. That is more than should be expected of us. If we are to keep our heads above water, float in the mainstream, a little dishonesty should be allowed.

Steering away from the basic truth not only is a sedate and easy way out, but also it is a thoughtful and considerate gesture toward those who concern themselves with us. Take, for example, the stock query of all time, "How are you?" If we were to answer that truthfully, we would not be making someone happy.

One day, feeling a need to reach out and touch someone, a friend called her daughter-in-law. Rather than unload her dreary feelings, she said, "My calendar for the next few weeks is so full . . . should you try to reach me . . ." Pitiful? Not at all. It had been a pleasant interlude, she'd contrived a little fib, and no one was harmed.

If you see a man with his hair parted an inch above one ear, you know he's hiding something. On the other hand, if he steps into a barbershop and says, "Shave off the top, baldness doesn't bother me one bit," you know he's whistling in the dark. Either way, he's not being quite honest.

Do you know someone who thinks short shorts are unflattering? Do you know someone who tsk-tsks at low-cut necklines because they leave nothing to the imagination? Someone who says false eyelashes and long, bouncy hair are tawdry? Someone who says she never liked these "floozy" trends at any age?

I do. I know her all too well. Her legs are dappled, her

upper arms are flabby, false eyelashes make her appear sleepy, and if she were to try any of these, well . . . no imagination could stretch so far. She's a faker.

I know a man who won't get out on a dance floor because (a) no one could dance to that kind of music, (b) he's wearing cork-soled shoes, or (c) his wife gets jealous if he dances with other women. The truth is, he can't part his hair without getting short of breath.

Some people back away from certain foods—too much salt, too many calories, or it causes heartburn. Raw vegetables and corn on the cob are rejected because they haven't the teeth for it. Yet they never level with any of these very good reasons. They would rather pretend they could eat it if they wanted to.

Actually, what we are all saying is, "No sad songs for me."

I have this young neighbor named Lorna. Lorna knows more about old age than anyone her age has a right to know.

"I just can't wait for you to meet my mother," she said to me one day. "You won't believe it."

"What won't I believe?" I asked as if I didn't already know.

"That she's my mother. She looks so young!"

"Compared to whom?"

"Compared to anyone her age."

"You mean she tells her age?"

"Why not? But wait 'til you see her."

I can wait. As a mother whose children depict her as "a good woman who irons her dish towels," I find this kind of conversation revolting.

Women who truly look their age find refuge in silence. They don't want that statistic breathed, much less whispered. But the woman who does not look her age wants it shouted, and her motive is obvious. She has come to know what will follow: the unbelieving listener is sure to come through with, "*What* is your secret?" This must be her finest hour.

I wish I had started a self-preservation program when I was young. The day Edna Wallace Hopper's Wrinkle-Free

Over What Hill? 105

went off the market is the day I should have switched to Oil of Olay. There comes a day when you know it is futile to try to strike back at what the years have cost you. How do you know when it's too late?

It's too late when you do facial exercises, and the bones move while the flesh just hangs there.

It's too late when the circles under your eyes are darker than your mascara.

It's too late when you find you can pinch more than an inch—on your neck.

It's too late when your concealer stick wears down faster than your lipstick.

And when you have tried first one, then another, and still another line of cosmetics, and the results are all the same, you know it is too late.

So we accept. We don't like it, but we accept it. And one thing is for sure, no one honestly can say that we didn't try.

We move along from passive acceptance to solemn resignation to deliberate avoidance to grim determination. And always we are dutiful. Each of us, in our own way, is trying to live up to whatever it is that "society" expects of us in any given year. But the thing to be remembered here is that when you have seen one old person, you have not seen them all.

No doubt you've read about the seventy-four-year-old grandmother who parachuted from a small plane flying at an altitude of 3,000 feet to a flawless landing.

There's another grandmother, a pistol-packin' grandmother, who heads up her city's auto crime department. And a ninety-four-year-old who celebrated eighty years as a Red Cross worker.

Recently I read about a ninety-two-year-old gentleman who is completing his doctoral dissertation in history. Another, at the age of eighty-two, is still active in business and says he can't wait to get up in the morning because every day is a challenge. Now this kind of drive I have never had. Wearing a dab of lavender eyeshadow is about as daring as I ever get. I don't even know anyone with that kind of energy.

I do have one friend who is risking life and limb learning all over again to walk in high heels.

A couple of my peers are jogging—sort of.

A few of us have let our hair grow a little longer. It's a rather nice feeling—that Gatsby look—for the second time around.

Seeing someone else perform the impossible has never been a challenge to me. I'm much more likely to throw in the towel than to throw down the gauntlet. Such was my feeling one evening as I watched from the sidelines while twenty or more extremely mature couples waltzed around a gym floor. Wayne King would have applauded them.

Later that same evening, when the band struck up "Five Foot Two, Eyes of Blue," one couple leaped from their chairs and all but cracked their kneecaps in an unconvincing demonstration of the Charleston. When they returned to their table, they gasped, "Is there anyone here who took a CPR course?"

"What do you think?" asked the young man who was their social director.

"I think they're a bunch of daredevils," I answered.

"No way," he shouted above the music. "They're as free as the breeze. No stress, no responsibilities, no demands. Their life's work is done. So they dance!"

One day "society" puts us on the shelf at age sixty. The next thing we know, we're being shamed into trying something new and spectacular.

Yet some of us need to know that we aren't what we once were. Some of us have been forced into facing some changes. Psyching ourselves into fantasies is not the answer.

For each of us there was, or will be, a last time for everything.

I once heard a child ask her grandmother, "Were you surprised the morning you woke up old?" If the question was amusing, the answer was hilarious.

"Oh, darling," her grandmother replied, "it wasn't like that at all. People don't become old just overnight."

The heck they don't. I know some grandmothers are apt storytellers, but that's a fairy tale if ever I heard one.

Sure, right from the moment we are born, we grow older each day. We reach the ages of twenty, thirty, forty, and even fifty—it's all in the process of growing older. We're still on our way and everybody's doing it.

It is when we become the finished product that the bomb falls. Suddenly we are there, and it *is* a surprise.

When was the last time you took off for anywhere on the run? I mean a lively sprint. When was the last time you took off for anywhere, in any fashion, without thinking twice?

When did dinner candles cease to be exotic and become only exasperating? When was the last time you practiced your come-hither look in front of a mirror?

There was one day when everything was fun, but it was back-to-back to a day when so little was. There was that one last day when you could eat a smorgasbord of your favorite fare with never a kickback.

Between the growing-older days and the being-older days, there was a last time for all these. We can't sift through our yesterdays and screen out the exact dates. We didn't know then that they were days to be remembered. If there were indications of what lurked ahead, either we chose to ignore them or we were too busy to notice.

So they went by and we just moved along. That's why we say things like, "it seems only yesterday," "time was when I could," and "if I'd known then what I know now."

There must have been a day when I could sing a song in key. If someone had told me that would be the last time I could do that, I would have practiced every day.

I wonder when I turned my last cartwheel, and why was it the last one? I should have kept trying day after day.

There was that last time for many things that I loved. I wish I'd tried just a little harder to hang in there. I would have, had I known then what I know now.

So that, I think, is what happened to a lot of us who can't be Senior Achievers. But somewhere out there, somewhere between the cockpit and the rocking chair, there is a little niche for each of us.

So let's hear it for all the gardeners, the golfers, the fishermen, the backyard cooks. Three cheers for those of you who are crocheting afghans, being surrogate grandparents, and walking a half-mile a day.

If we accomplish nothing else, we are letting it be known that grandparents aren't just for baby-sitting anymore.

Shakespeare wrote a great deal about the insights and fears of the aged, but not much on the compensations and pleasures. In *Much Ado About Nothing* he wrote, "A good old man will be talking, as they say, 'When the age is in, the wit is out.' "

I never understood half of what William Shakespeare was saying, but he was right as rain on that first part. Surely good old men (and good old ladies) do love to visit.

Whenever two or more oldies are gathered together, whatever the occasion, sooner or later the conversation will turn to the good old days. Never is it the *bad* old days.

You and I know there were some bad old days, don't we? Some of the worst bad old days were during the Great Depression. Those were the hungry years—a time when poverty was a way of life. But we don't dwell on that. Instead we talk about how two and three families lived under one roof. How we were drawn closer together, and how, as a strong people, we pulled ourselves out of it.

One evening I overheard a man telling about a house that he'd built for $3,500. "Boy, what I mean, that house was *built*," he said. "That house had everything anybody could ever want." He speculated on what that same house would be worth on today's market.

I remember that house. It had one bathroom, and I've seen more attractive ones in gas stations.

Several others had similar tales to tell, but no one seemed to recall the years we were caught up in Florida Fever. It's still a little painful to talk about the bad old day we bought a plot of ground from a blueprint.

Some of us like to tell how we "didn't even know what a baby-sitter was, for heaven's sake. We took our kids everywhere. Wherever we went, they went. It was fun for all of us."

Sure, starting out with our little kids, all in their Sunday best, each of them full of promises of good behavior, was fun. But lugging them home at day's end all sleepy and sticky and readying them for bed is the part we don't talk about.

We look back on Sunday picnics in the park as the summer's highlights. Everyone attended, everyone entered the contests, and everyone loved everyone. No one ever sprained an ankle in the three-legged races, no boat ever overturned, no one gossiped, the kids never fought with each other—and the *food!* Well, women just don't cook like that any more.

If anyone were to remind us that we drank warm lemonade, ate soupy potato salad, and spent half the next day rubbing lemon juice into grass-stained clothes, we'd say, "I swear I don't remember anything like that happening, ever."

So, that's the way we are. We delude ourselves with the afterglow. What may have been unpleasant then is simply unimportant now.

At our age, comfort is what we want. And forgetting that it ever, ever rained on our parade is most comfortable.

We aren't always so adept at seeing the bright side, however. Sometimes we think there must be thirty hours in every day and eight days in every week and that finding enough busy work to fill them becomes darn wearisome.

We say there's not much to look forward to, and we have little fervor for what there is—and we see our horizons narrowing.

We say we bump into our spouse in the hall, and we accuse each other of mumbling—and the house seems to get bigger each year.

We say there are too many days when we should have stayed in bed, and too many things we can't eat—and too many memories that we can't erase.

We say there's no longer a place in our life for advancement, and there are no more goals—and nothing left to fight for.

We say taxes went up again, and our pension check didn't—and our congressman is sitting out there doing nothing.

We say we're sick of walking the same old paths,

fishing the same old streams, and reading the same old guff.

We say our kids are living mighty high off the hog and our grandchildren don't know a dime from a dollar—and they're all headed for one big surprise when the bottom drops out.

We say the old *zing* is gone, and no one wants to benefit from our experiences—and we think it won't be long until we're put out to pasture.

Yes, sometimes we say these things. Sometimes there is a desire for martyrdom in our subconscious. And sometimes it is the things we read and hear that throw us into a blue funk.

Listed in a scientific study of a couple years ago among the future trends we might expect was "Lengthening lifespans will mean more and more elderly Americans." Although we could have figured this out for ourselves, for a minute we found this encouraging. Further on, however, we read, "Social Security officials are concerned about the strain that will be imposed as more and more elderly draw benefits." Today they are even more concerned. In fact, they are downright sick about it.

A more current article stated that Americans are taking better care of themselves today than ever before, and the level of health in this country is good and getting better. They even cited some of the elderly as survivors. Now I ask you, is this good news or isn't it? It isn't. It's a problem. A problem to our government because they don't know how they are going to take care of such a large number of people who have lived too long.

The blame, it seems, falls on society. Society has "permitted" us to live longer than we were supposed to, and now there is great stress on the nation's health care resources.

Well, gee! Reading this made us sad. We were sorry to learn that we were the ones standing in the way of our country's economic recovery.

We didn't know that the average man was supposed to turn in his chips at age 69.5, or that the average woman was to check out when she reached her 77.2 birthday. We certainly never planned on becoming a bunch of reactionaries.

Over What *Hill?*

We've just been muddling along through these golden years thinking we'd earned these benefits.

We've tightened our belts before. We can do it again. If there is not the wherewithal to bring home care to those who need it, we'll go back to helping each other. We used to do a lot of that.

Forget those Senior Citizen bus trips. We've still got our jigsaw puzzles left over from 1929.

So, we snap back. We may be on the wrong side of fifty, our future goals may be limited, but when it comes to being shackled with threats and fears, *we have had it!*

We aren't expecting the sublime, but neither do we want the ridiculous. We don't want to be sorted out like chaff from the rest of the grain. And even when we are, don't string us up like a bunch of gingerbread men holding hands.

Just before I was to give a talk to a group of rather elderly people one evening, the program chairman pulled me aside to tell me something she felt I should know.

"These people," she whispered, "have difficulty sitting still for any length of time. Perhaps if you could assure them that you would not be offended if they got up and moved about while you are talking . . ."

At first I was inclined to go along with her. Surely I could comply with such a small request, but after scanning the audience, I had second thoughts.

They looked okay to me. None were sitting on the edge of their chairs. They appeared to be comfortably seated; I, on the other hand, would be standing the whole time. So I didn't give them an out. I figured if I could stand it, they should be able to.

There are still those who think that all of us have one foot in the ferryboat. I think I know how that happened. One time, for their program, this same group had a string ensemble. Halfway through the hour-long concert, one oldie in the audience left the room to go to the bathroom. Then, right away, you see, someone assumed that each and every one of them had a short attention span.

My own attention span is limited, but it's no shorter than it was fifty years ago. During lectures, sermons, and debates, you'll find me out in left field but, invite me to see *Fiddler on the Roof* for the seventh time, and I'll be waiting for you in the first row.

Aunt Cassie is very opinionated. I've told you how highhanded she can be when she visits us, but this is nothing new. That's why I sometimes lose patience with her. I can't say she has become a cantankerous old lady because she was a cantankerous *young* lady.

There's Janie, who pouts and even cries when she doesn't get her own way. Is she becoming childish? Assuredly not! I saw Janie pull the same wiles on her father that she is pulling on her husband today.

I suspect that, in consideration for the "old folks," well-meaning but overzealous individuals are trying to give some credence to our behavior.

Robert Browning took too much for granted when he wrote "Grow old along with me." I used to think that was the most beautiful verse I'd ever been forced to read.

Back then, I thought he was writing this to his wife, but later I learned she had died years before. So I don't know to whom he was making this proposition, but it doesn't matter because the romance has gone.

"Grow old along with me." What kind of an invitation is that anyway? If my husband couldn't come up with something better than that, I'd tell him to forget it.

One day after he'd finished cleaning the basement, Martin yelled in the back door. "Wanta' ride out to the dump with me?" I thought that was shabby.

I'm less than thrilled when he asks me to go fishing or to a ballgame. In the late winter when he suggests we ride down to the dam to see the ice break up, I don't exactly quiver with joy. The best offer I've had lately is, "How about getting some fresh air?"

I say okay to all of these. And it is okay. It's more than okay—it's a blessing to have a partner in these sunset years, but growing old is such an individual matter. I mean like when one of that partnership has a broken leg, the other does not necessarily have to have one, too.

It takes two to tango and two to start an argument.

Two may live as cheaply as one, and there's tea for two, but once we start down that thorny path of old age, the sweetheart parade is over.

No matter how mutual a relationship has been, regardless of how much we've relied on another—even if we have been the most clinging vine of them all—when it comes to growing old, we are very much on our own.

A popular theory, too, is one that says the elderly disapprove of much that is going on in the world today. They reckon that we are looking down from the Great Plateau and deeming everyone's lifestyle scandalous.

I suppose people of our generation should be shocked at some of the movies that are being made today. The one that was ballyhooed with I Want You to have My Baby surely did attract our attention.

I suppose we should touch our foreheads with the back of our hands, reel about, and sink into the nearest chair.

Maybe we should shake our heads and cluck our tongues and mutter, "Whatever is the world coming to?"

Not so! We are neither shocked nor dismayed. What we are is surprised. Surprised that everything has to be spelled out.

Are performers today so lacking in interpretive ability that they can't communicate without bellowing? Are viewers so unimaginative that they can't read between the lines?

When Rudolph Valentino peered out from under his turban with those heavy-lidded eyes, we got the message. At night when Vilma Banky was asleep; "into her tent he'd creep," and we knew they weren't in there writing love letters in the sand.

When Charles Boyer wanted to take Hedy Lamarr away to the Casbah, I knew he was up to no good. Not because he was a fugitive, but because of his facial expression, which fell somewhere between sinister and sickening.

There were, of course, some sticky-sweet lovebirds to whom we gave little thought. Nelson Eddy and Jeanette MacDonald, for example, never stopped singing long enough to settle down to anything serious.

Ruby Keeler and Dick Powell could have, and probably did, dance all night. And Janet Gaynor and Charles Farrell were in seventh heaven just holding hands.

But there were others like John Gilbert and Ronald Colman whose very countenances were suggestive. Hidden behind every pair of half-closed eyes, every pouty mouth, every twitching nostril, and every slithery movement was a lurid meaning.

Norma Shearer never announced she was going to change into something more comfortable. She was in something more comfortable at the beginning of the scene.

In *It Happened One Night*, Claudette Colbert and Clark Gable, forced to share a motel room, improvised a room divider. That was it. End of scene. We took it from there.

The movie industry in those days left a lot up to us. The viewer was his own censor. He could read in as much sensuality as he chose. Or he could mentally blue-pencil whatever he thought distasteful. I doubt there was ever much left on the mind's eye cutting room floor.

We weren't shocked then. We aren't now.

So that's the way it is. Some of us slip into old age as we would into a warm coat. Others go kicking and screaming all the way. Those who quietly accept will be depicted on Mother's and Father's Day cards for years to come. Those who put up a fight will forever be remembered as absurd. I will be one of the absurd.

Don't ask us to describe the view from the other side of the hill; we aren't over it—not yet.

Keepsakes of My Mind

I have been accused of living in the past. Not fair. I do *write* of the past but with very good reason. It's far better than anything I can dream up for the future.

Yet I must confess there are times, when I am in a self-demeaning mood, I feel guilty for the time I spend daydreaming. I think I am wasting precious hours in idle thoughts—hours that might be better spent waving a flag or standing on a soap box.

Then I tell myself that this kind of thinking is silly. I've paid my dues. I've earned the luxury of doing nothing. Now I am a retiree and retirees are supposed to enjoy some leisure time. We've even been dubbed The New Leisure Class, for heaven's sake!

If I learn anything from thinking about the past, it is inadvertent. That is not my intention. My mind calls up remembrances randomly. I never know what will appear on my imaginary screen. If it is a memory that does not give me pleasure, I switch channels.

My thoughts do not flow in any structured sequence. In fact, they don't flow at all. They simply crop up, one after another, with little or no connection.

And so I ponder.

RADIO

Our first radio was a crystal set with one set of earphones. My father would slip them on and manipulate the three dials while we watched, hoping upon hope that he'd get something. The second he said, "I think I've got Shreveport!" we'd all start scrambling for the earphones. Each of us would listen in turn, patiently waiting to hear a voice or a few notes of music through the shrieks and screeches, which we learned to call static.

Progress, though, was just around the corner. Soon we discovered that by setting the earphones in a dishpan, the sound would reverberate, allowing all of us to hear at the same time. So, out of the dishpan in the center of the living room came the voices of Graham McNamee, the Cliquot Club Eskimos, and the A & P Gypsies.

My grandchildren can't believe there is more to radio than jukebox hits. They are amazed when I tell them how even *their* parents once sat around a radio listening to "Let's Pretend."

When I told them that their grandfather and I listened to "Gunsmoke" on radio for years, they asked, "Didn't you wonder what Matt Dillon looked like?"

I thought for a moment, then answered, "No, we didn't wonder at all. We knew. At least, we thought we knew. You see we formed our own picture of each character."

Radio gave its listeners a title, a plot, dialogue, and sound effects and trusted them to be enterprising enough to put it all together.

When "Ma Perkins" gave us a fast-sell spiel for her vegetable shortening, we pictured her right there in her kitchen, elbow deep in flour.

If "One Man's Family" opened with "Father and Mother Barbour have just seated themselves at the breakfast table," we envisioned a flowered lunch cloth, yellow dishes, sun streaming through crisscross curtains, and this model, paper doll family around the table.

We did our own casting of characters. We were uncommitted and could change the picture to suit our liking. It was make-believe. It was magic.

Keepsakes of My Mind

Television has robbed us of this. Because we see actors in the same role over long periods of time, they make an impression that is not easily erased.

For example, when my favorite, happily married soap opera character appeared during the show's break puckering her wet lips and making sensual overtures toward a strange man, I had misgivings.

Remember when Raymond Burr had that long run as "Perry Mason?" We were still watching it in reruns when he appeared in a wheel chair in "Ironside." The transition was too abrupt. People were saying, "What happened to old Perry? Did he have an accident?"

Oh, sure, TV has more than these to offer. We've been eyewitnesses to history in the making. We have seen coronations, inaugurations, Super Bowls, and royal weddings. Its cameras have taken us to the bottom of the ocean and to the surface of the moon. We have been privileged to a peek behind heretofore closed doors.

Magic? Not really. You see, when we press a button these days, we expect something to happen—and it better be good.

PERISH SUCH THOUGHTS

At a meeting some time ago, the moderator tossed out this question: "If you had it to do all over again, what would you do differently?"

As though she had been waiting for this moment, one woman said, "I would never have had any children." (I shuddered.)

And just as spontaneously, another said, "Right! With no children, there would be no grandchildren to worry about today, and that would be a dividend." (I quaked.)

With icebreakers like these, the moderator could have donned her bonnet and walked out. There was no need for prompting. There was an aura of we-thought-you'd-never-ask as the answers came thick and fast.

"If I had it to do all over again, I'd be defiant," said one man. "I'd have stood my ground with my parents."

"I'd have lived a life of detachment. As I grew up, I'd have left behind aunts, uncles, cousins – yes, even brothers and sisters. I'd have concentrated on Number One!"

"I would have placed less importance on *things*. I wish I hadn't accumulated *things* to which I've become attached, then I could have been a wanderer with nothing to fence me in."

I had a mental list of some changes I might make, had I the chance to do it all over again. Like on my first day as a housewife, I would have feigned a serious allergy to *all* oven cleaners, including those that work while I sleep.

At a very early age, I would have cultivated a passion for dandelions and a strong aversion to yellow roses.

I would not have handed that poor little kid in the supermarket parking lot one whole dollar for a surprise package (stale cookies), had I known his father owned the store.

I'd have allowed my children to "get by" with at least half as much as my grandchildren do.

And I would never have attended this meeting had I known I would be such a misfit.

How could anyone be so open? They seemed filled with resentments. Wow! The things they said. But they were honest, they did have courage, they did lay it right on the line. Maybe they felt better than I did right then.

But I couldn't have said the things they said. Even if I'd shared their feelings, I couldn't have. Lordy, I'd be afraid that someday I'd have to *pay* for having such thoughts.

I guess having a grandmother who believed in leprechauns left its mark.

ELECTION DAY

My parents weren't the partying kind, but once every four years family and friends were invited to our home for an Election Day party.

In those earlier years, we children nestled down midst the guests' coats and wraps, which had been tossed onto a

Keepsakes of My Mind

bed. Lying crosswise, we would giggle and whisper until one by one we fell asleep.

Out in the living room, the grown-ups played whist and flinch, and always there was the Ouija board. "Who will be our next president?" they would ask. Because "as Maine goes, so goes the nation" was their only yardstick, they would say, "Tell me, Ouija, how will the state of Maine go?"

After a time, the ladies would go into the kitchen to help my mother serve lunch. For them the victory lay not only in which candidate won, but in the fact that they, as women, were newly franchised voters. For the first time they were playing a part in a big decision.

Late in the evening, the menfolks would put on their coats and walk down to the newspaper office to see if anything was pasted on the window or if the special edition was out.

Often they returned unenlightened, and after several such trips, they picked up their sleeping children and left, knowing it might be morning before they would learn the outcome.

In later years, with the advent of radio and its nationwide networks, the election party was enlivened. There was no place for conversation or games as everyone gathered around this latest bit of magic and mystery.

The same airwaves that brought them Jessica Dragonette and Moran and Mack also would bring them the election results at whirlwind speed.

From the man who led them through a European war to the man who gave out love to the man who was afraid to rock the boat, these good people went to the polls and embraced their citizenship.

Their hope and trust was never shaken as they moved from the president, who on his last day in office said, "We are at the end of our string" to the man for whom no one had lukewarm feelings, because you either loved or hated him.

Because of the way my birthday fell, I was nearly twenty-four years old before I could vote in a presidential election. When, at last, I did qualify, I was exhilarated; I felt it was a privilege to cast my vote.

I still do.

FULL CIRCLE

The day the telephone company installed a *dial* phone in my grandmother's home was the day she placed her last telephone call. She had been very happy with the old one, and she wasn't about to go along with something that would eventually put a lot of good people out of work.

No amount of explaining or cajoling would change her mind. Although we took turns dialing for her, we never let her forget how silly it was.

Some time ago I had my first encounter with a computerized bank teller. As I stood there reading the instructions that, if I did it right, would give me instant access to any account in my name, I became aware of other customers waiting their turn.

Deciding it would be far simpler to return the next day when the bank was open, I put my card back in my purse and walked away. It was then I remembered Grandma and her dial telephone. It was then I felt the first bit of compassion for her.

During a turbulent plane trip, I found myself grasping the armrests. I can't say I saw my whole life flashing before me, but I did recall a lady who, many years ago, clung to the seat cushions while riding in a touring car over bumpy dirt roads. We had laughed and said, "What good would it do her if the car rolled over?" Now I understood her fright and tightened my grip on the armrests.

Understanding and discernment are sometimes a long time coming.

Someone suggested that youth and insensitivity go hand in hand. I can't buy that. I think it's that age-old truism about having to walk in someone else's shoes. That's what is coming to the surface here.

Today I can see through a lot of things.

Today I can appreciate another's mood and top it with one of my own.

High time. Long overdue.

Keepsakes of My Mind

ANOTHER DOOR CLOSES

One year our child was the only preschooler in the block. All summer she had been one of the neighborhood moppets—a happy partaker in all their fun and games. She could perform a headstand as well as the next one.

At the age of four and one-half, she opened her own lemonade stand. She had been so busy throughout those fun-filled summer days.

Then fall arrived. School doors opened, and her friends marched through. When the doors closed, she was on the outside. She was not quite five.

She'd been told she must wait another year to start school. She knew she had not reached the magical age, and she knew that these children would be starting school and she would not. What she did not know is what it would be like.

She couldn't know she would be the only kid on the block that Labor Day weekend without a pencil box. She couldn't know that there would be no little people around all day long after that. When she stepped outside to play—well, she'd just never known such quietness. So she dressed her dog in doll clothes, sat on a kitchen stool and fidgeted, and watched for the other children to return from school.

Here again, she couldn't know that they'd be bringing home newly acquired friends, nor that they would be all involved in work sheets—and what was this thing called show and tell?"

Reaching the age of sixty-plus may not be as magical as reaching the school age, but for most of us, it is another beginning. We have held up our end of a work load and fought the good fight. We mingled, joined, welcomed, and sometimes struggled. We knew that some time at or about this age, we would be giving up our life's work. Yet we couldn't know what it would be like.

During those first months of idleness, we watched while the rest of the world rolled by. The early morning surge of traffic as friends and neighbors left for work was followed by day-long stillness. We looked forward to their return from work at day's end, but it wasn't the same.

We no longer were a part of their kind of days. The nearness was gone. Our summer days had passed and autumn was upon us. A door had been closed—and we were on the outside. So we fidgeted for a time, some of us longer than others.

There were those who happily anticipated rest and relaxation. Some had trouble letting go of the reins, whereas others climbed out of the driver's seat and then tried to crawl back in. None of us could know what it really would be like.

AS I WAS SAYING...

I wish I had a flair for attracting attention. Oh, I know there are ways. I could turn up at some affair wearing an unmatched pair of earrings. I could dash to the mailbox wearing Martin's windbreaker over my housecoat. In church I could twist an ankle at the communion rail—but I've done all those. Anyway, that's not what I mean.

I don't look for anyone to be smitten by me. There was a time, long ago, when I pictured myself descending a staircase into the waiting arms of Warner Baxter. I gave that up when we moved into a basement house, and I found myself coming up the stairs to join Chubby Blash and his Hupmobile. No, I do not expect ever to perform in a way that will draw the multitudes.

All I want today—all I have ever wanted—is the ability to wriggle my way into a conversation. All I crave is one little moment of time to say what I have to say.

For years I have watched others manipulate a conversation to their advantage. They need only to rest a hand on the shoulder next to their own and the floor is theirs. For me, it doesn't work. I've tried "ahem" and "pst, pst," and the most I get is a sidelong glance.

I remember one occasion when I was sure the little tale I had in mind would fit in with the flow. I took a deep breath, swallowed a time or two, wet my lips, and started. "Yesterday morning I was cleaning the cupboard under the sink . . ."

Keepsakes of My Mind

"Don't you hate that job?" one of them asked.

When finally they had agreed that yes, they hated that job, someone looked at her watch. The party was over, and so was my moment.

Maybe, I thought, I don't preface my comments interestingly enough. Perhaps I should start with something more picturesque than the kitchen sink. Or better yet, something that would really grab them.

I thought I was ready. "Sometimes at night," I began, "when I hear the rain against my windowpane, I lean back and think about that summer so long ago when we . . . "

"I know what you're going to tell," one of them screamed. Then between hysterics, they took turns telling my story. When finally they had lapped up all the meaty, choice tidbits, they tossed the dry bone back to me.

As I sat there in the earsplitting silence staring at the floor, someone said, "Go ahead, Helen. What were you going to say?"

"She's offended," I heard another whisper. "We're sorry."

More silence as I continued staring at the floor. Any anger I'd felt was leaving, but it was too late. I'd forgotten what I was going to say.

LET ME BE THE LAST

Some people are so courageous. They can meet a challenge head-on. Dauntlessly they go through life allowing little, if anything, to strike them as awesome.

Then there are those who are timid, overanxious. Fearful of what may be just around the corner, they stick to the middle of the road. I fall into this latter group—but with a slight twist. I am, basically, all these things, but I try to conceal it. I am a bluffer.

Like the father who buys his son an electric train because he himself wants it, so my father bought me a horse when I was five years old. The terror I felt was equaled only by my father's love for it. He set me astride the animal and took my picture. Today that picture would be cause enough for someone to charge my father with child abuse. Nothing but panic shone from my eyes, but my mouth was half-smiling.

A woman came to my door one day, selling a religious pamphlet. As I took the paper and handed her a coin, she said, "At *our* age, we need all the help we can get for the little time that is left us." Because I was going into the hospital the next morning for surgery, Martin said, "Well, now, that was unfortunate."

I said, "Forget it! I don't believe in *omens!*" I don't? Then why did her words ring in my ears until the anesthetic took over?

When we go fishing alone, Martin baits the hooks. But if we're with a party, I do my own. As I lace the worm on the hook, I make believe it's a piece of yarn, and the hook, a crochet hook. I stare in disbelief when another woman puts her hand into the minnow pail. When I forced myself to do the same, the minnow looked up at me.

The first plane trip I ever took was in one of those little three-passenger deals where you step on the wing as you climb in. For one cent per pound of your weight, you got a couple swings over the city, and a charity got the money. I'd have signed up for six months of tithing if I could have backed out.

As we left the ground, I said to the pilot (just testing to see if I had any breath), "This must get pretty boring for you." He yawned and answered, "Yeah—but I need the practice." If he'd kicked me in the stomach, my inner reaction could not have been worse.

What's wrong with a child, boy or girl, admitting he/she is afraid of a horse? Why should anyone feel any shame because they've allowed another's remark get to them?

Why should I feel that because one woman handles a fly-rod like a pro, I, too, must excel. As for the plane ride, I still think I was a little zany to get into that rattletrap.

I look at my grandchildren and hope I am the last of the Great Pretenders.

Keepsakes of My Mind

MY GRANDPARENTS WERE VERY HEALTHY

If there is one married couple living today that claims they have never had a squabble, I don't want to meet them. If their lives have been that dull, what's there to tell?

One woman says the only basis for contention in her marriage has been their offspring. I don't swallow that. Neither can I go along with, "Our spats are the result of the way our parents raised us."

Disputes do arise from a difference of opinions but they stem from much less obvious roots. One way to avoid them is never to have an opinion, and wouldn't that be a cheery existence? The other choice is to clam up, which is equally boring but more aggravating.

One afternoon while watching TV, I asked myself, "What is it about these soaps that makes them so unbelievable?" Then it came to me—they don't show enough family quarrels. They cheat, lust, bribe, embezzle, and even kill, but they never have a good, practical squabble.

Why not, I wonder. We are told that this outpouring of feelings is good for us. It is a healthy practice. It is a release, and we are better off for it. All I can add is that my grandparents must have been a very relieved and healthy little pair.

I remember my grandfather being very owlish one day when I was staying with them, and my grandmother had minced no words in telling him so. Grandpa lashed back with a tirade of expletives all directed toward someone called Volstead.

Grandma said that if she could live through wheatless Tuesdays, she guessed he could get along without his schnapps, and Grandpa said that ever since Grandma found out she could vote, she'd been mighty mouthy.

This was about all I heard because I was sitting on the porch steps, and they were inside. When I came in, Grandpa had put on his shirt, Grandma had changed her apron, and we all sat down to the table and said our prayers.

My parents, too, sometimes exchanged peppery words. The day Papa returned home from work and saw Mama with her hair bobbed was one of a kind. He had only begun to recover when the second bomb fell. She had it cut in a *man's* barbershop!

I'm not one bit ashamed that in our family there have been some fine, sparkling, and vigorous verbal battles.

I think it proves we are normal.

THIS IS NOT A RECORDING

When I answered my telephone one morning, I heard a voice say, "Are you an answering service?"

I said, "Well, not really." Then a click, then the dial tone.

Again my phone rang. And again "Are you an answering service?"

"No, I tried to tell you that." Click. Dial tone.

Again, and now it was time to answer a question with a question. I said, "Are *you* a recording?" Click. Dial tone.

Is this progress? Are these the unnecessary calls that stand in the way of better service at the lowest possible cost? Is this the tomorrow we thought would be better than yesterday?

I remember when the question was not "What's your number?" but "Do you have a telephone?" Asking "Are you in the book?" was needless. Land sakes, if we were lucky enough to have a telephone, we certainly wanted to be listed in the directory.

My grandparents' telephone number was Humboldt 3469. That was because they lived in a city. Big numbers like that were used only in big towns. Where I lived, we had two-digit numbers followed by a color—36 White, 84 Black, and 79 Red. The color designated the section of the town.

We referred to the operator as Central and rightfully so because she was the heart of that bewildering maze of wires that kept us in touch. Agnes never clicked us off in the middle of a sentence.

We lifted the receiver on our phone and said, "Central, ring 42 White for me, please." While she was ringing the number, she might say, "Need rain, don't we?" Or another time it might be, "If it's Clara you want to talk to, I just saw her walk by here."

Once I recall placing a call to Seattle. "Agnes," I said, "I want to talk to my brother out in Washington."

"Can you give me a minute here to clear this board? When I get him on the line, I'll ring you right back. How is Jerry?"

Agnes performed a more somber kind of service, too. When the voice on the other end was muffled and boozy, she knew it was the village inebriate and would send a taxi for him. She detected emergencies instinctively and would ring the fire department, the police station, or the hospital.

Sometimes Agnes's "Number please?" was garbled because she was eating her lunch, and there were times when we waited and waited for her to return from the restroom. Yet there was a homey alliance, a warm and personal contact. Central was out there, alive and well.

THE DEPOT

I grew up in a little town where the railroad was heart and hub. Those were days when the trains went everywhere, when steam power was unchallenged, and there was a steady, rhythmic sound to the engine.

We had no swimming pool or stadium. No portion of our one park was set aside for playground equipment, and no one ever saw the need for devising girls' or boys' clubs to keep us out of trouble. Were we bored? At loose ends? Never—because we had a train station. We could always walk down to the depot.

Inside people paced across the dark, oiled wooden floors. Others stood in line to buy their tickets. We children would scoot back and forth on the benches and sometimes put a penny in the candy machine and get two Chicklets in return. Finally the station agent would slam down the ticket window and put on his hat, and we would follow him outside. The train was coming.

Until this moment there was a hushed atmosphere. Now the activity increased. Luggage and mail carts were rolled out, and there were loud voices as people crowded and pushed along the platform. Then, what excitement as the train who-o-o-shed to a stop! The "old 52" was on time, and all was right with the world.

The arriving passengers stepped slowly from the train, scanning the crowd for familiar faces. Others, impatient and eager, waited to board.

Trains. They brought us our food and our mail, our cousins and our grandmothers and once – sometimes twice – a year, they brought us the circus. I was fascinated with it all, but even more memorable were the whistles.

It has been said that a locomotive engineer ran the train by the seat of his pants. This may be, but there was much more to his job. He didn't blow that whistle just to give us a thrill. No, indeed.

When we heard that one long blast, he was telling us that he was approaching a station. Ever alert for crossings, he sounded two longs, one short, and one long. Three short toots meant he was backing up, and two shorts meant "all aboard!"

There was also the shop whistle, loud and commanding. Three times each day we heard that, and housewives set their clocks and their tables by it.

During a press conference, Ronald Reagan, in an effort to convincingly establish his understanding of the working man, said, "We lived so close to the railroad tracks, we could hear the whistle real loud."

Mr. President, sir, that wasn't a hardship. That was an advantage.

ANOTHER TIME

I look back to a time – another time – when washing machines had wringers and a shoe repair shop did a thriving business, a time when aprons were made from flour sacks, and ladies spent a companionable afternoon hemming tea towels made from sugar sacks. I remember the things we did for amusement.

Sundays meant wearing your best dress and scrambling for the funny papers – Andy Gump and the Katzenjammer

Keepsakes of My Mind

Kids. It was aunts, uncles, and cousins coming for dinner, and the spiced peaches that were brought out only for this special day.

Playing an even bigger part in our entertainment were the things that came to town – the circus, the carnival, the Chautauqua, and Santa Claus, Then there was the movie theater with its fifteen-cent matinees, in which the boy next door came to the girl's rescue just in the nick of time and the villain was foiled again.

Oh, the times we had. How fanciful.

I dwell on a time when every schoolroom had a cloakroom, and every desk, an inkwell. It was a time when teachers boarded and roomed in private homes, and I thought they were a breed set apart from the rest of us.

I recall with distaste the tiny cloth sack of asafetida we wore on a string around the neck to ward off germs. Still with me is the sense of timidity I felt for the truant officer who could, at the least provocation, throw me in jail (and my father with me).

Oh, the things we believed. How gullible.

Frequently my mind visits another time when homes had porches and screened doors that slammed. When locomotives had cowcatchers, and automobiles had running boards and rumble seats.

This was a time when being popular carried more weight than flaunting the assertions of a new era. So, as is true in each generation, we conformed by adopting slangy expressions – "hot diggity" and "ain't we got fun."

Life was either "hotsy-totsy" or "horsefeathers." We spoke of the war that was to have ended all wars and were glad we'd escaped it. It was at this time that we heard rumblings of hard times ahead, and we had an answer for that: "Watch our nickels and the dollars will take care of themselves."

Oh, the things we said. How unknowing.

CAN THIS HISTORY BE REPEATED?

Athough it puts a strain on the imagination, there really was a time when:

Missing a train was no big deal because there would be another the next day, same time, same destination.

I had to connive, bribe, and beg for a little quiet, uninterrupted time.

The butcher handed me a quarter's worth of beefsteak without my specifying any special cut, and I'd fry it without asking rare or medium.

Motorists honked their horns when passing another car and when meeting ones from their home states.

We bought bread unwrapped and unsliced.

Drugstores had soda fountains, but did not sell T-shirts, house plants, or pots and pans.

A heater in a new car was considered an "extra" and, therefore, was optional.

Nationwide news could be *viewed* only at the movies between the first and second shows.

Capable and trustworthy baby-sitters were available for thirty-five cents an evening.

Smog was not in the air, our vocabulary, or the dictionary.

Al Jolson singing "Sonny Boy" was a real tearjerker, melodrama at its finest.

With four little words—"Wanna buy a duck?"—Joe Penner could produce comedy of belly-laugh dimension.

Happiness was a report card boasting an *E* in deportment and effort.

Sadness was midnight and the band playing "Goodnight Sweetheart."

Security was paying as you go, living within one's means. Easy credit and deferred payments were only brainstorms of newfangled economists.

Unbelievable! In no way can we envision a return of this kind of life.

Yet when I recall H. V. Kaltenborn's daily report on Hitler's progress—how we listened, unsure about whether there was nothing to fear but fear itself—I worry. Sometimes history does repeat itself.

Keepsakes of My Mind

HAPPY YOUTH AND A VANILLA COKE

Of all the freedoms we enjoy, the least exploited and perhaps the most relished is the freedom to think. One day not so long ago, I wallowed in this freedom. Walking down the main street of a small river town, I looked through a drugstore window and saw myself in a very large mirror. Could it be? Could it possibly be? It could. It was. A really truly, honest-to-goodness soda fountain. Original and unspoiled. Gleaming, sparkling, and beckoning.

Inside the store, I pulled myself onto one of the counter stools and said, "Do you make Cokes? I mean do those faucets actually work?"

The girl behind the counter smiled. "They sure do. What flavor?"

"Vanilla?" I ventured, not believing my luck.

In minutes she set the frosty glass before me. No can. No bottle. Leaning forward to reach the straw, I took my first sip. It had been a long time since I'd tasted anything quite so yummy. At the same time, I caught my reflection in the mirror, and it was at this point that giddiness overtook me.

My hair was red again. It was curly again, and I didn't care a whit that it was windblown. My hands were plump, with no veins showing. No brown spots. I was wearing a pleated skirt, and I had an apple in my sweater pocket.

One of my shoestrings was knotted where it had broken that morning. I'd lost the key to my locker and had been late for basketball practice. I'd skipped my chemistry class, bought a cream twist at the bakery, then walked to the top of the hill, where I stood eating it in the shelter of the old water tower.

I could read the marquee on the theaters across the street: Joan Crawford in *Our Dancing Daughters*. Next to it was S. S. Kresge, and on the corner, Standard Oil. Their sign boasted that this was one of their 1,000 stations.

On the magazine stand in front of the United Cigar

Store were *Colliers, True Confessions, Country Gentleman,* and the *Literary Digest.* On my way home, I would stop at the music shop and see if they had any new sheet music, and I'd take another look at the ukuleles.

Mama would have supper started, and I should be there to set the table. Last night we got KDKA Pittsburgh on the radio. Maybe tonight I'd listen in again . . . unless some kids stopped by . . . or somebody could get his dad's car.

I lifted the straw from the glass and drained it of the last piece of crushed ice. As I reached for a nickel in my purse, I heard someone say, "That will be sixty cents."

Sixty cents for a vanilla Coke? A bargain any day.

POSTSCRIPT

These things that come to my mind out of the past are always so very immaterial.

During my lifetime I have seen wars, depression, inflation, a moon landing, epidemics, and medical breakthroughs. But this doesn't stop me from wondering why I never see Four-B brand canned goods on the shelves any more.

Throughout the years, some beautiful people have touched my life. I am grateful and will never forget them. At the same time, I would like to recall the name of that kid in grade school who took the hard-boiled egg from her lunch pail and cracked it on my head.

I have not traveled far and wide, but neither have I been glued to one spot. I have seen oceans, mountains, deserts, citrus groves, vineyards, cotton fields, and sky-blue waters. Yet I keep thinking about a farm I visited as a child. There were other children there, as well as a barn, a shed, and a house with geraniums planted in tomato cans in the window.

There are a lot of things we don't see any more. So much is lost in the passing of the years, but I do think about them.

Do you remember when a man on his way to the barbershop would say, "I'm going to get my ears set out?"

How long has it been since you sewed up a runner in a silk stocking, smoothed your iron with melted paraffin, and shampooed with Mulsified Coconut Oil?

Personally, I can't remember the last time I saw a mother wheeling her child in a baby carriage.

I used to receive letters with SWAK on the outside of the envelope, but not any more.

Those of you who have never struggled with clinkers in a furnace, wringers on a washing machine, and shoelaces after the "tins" have fallen off won't know what I've been talking about.

But if you have eaten your lunch at a Ford-Hopkins Drugstore, if ever you ordered your groceries from a mail-order house, if you have emptied the drain pan from under the refrigerator, and if you were there when the syncopated sound of jazz moved northward out of New Orleans, then you don't need me. You have walked down this lane before.

But, gee – hasn't it been a long, long time?!